Change at Work:
Not Just Surviving but Thriving

Change at Work: Not Just Surviving but Thriving

Seema Rao

&

Robert J. Weisberg

First Edition: 2018

Library of Congress Cataloging-in-Publication Data
Rao, Seema and Weisberg, Robert J.
Change at Work: Not Just Surviving but Thriving/ Seema Rao and Robert J.
Weisberg-1st ED
p.cm.
ISBN 1979251185
1. Self-Help, Work 2. Professional Development

ISBN-13: 978-1979251181 ISBN-10: 1979251185

14 13 12 11 10 / 10 9 8 7 6 5 4 3 2 1

Dedications

RW—
To D, my change agent.
And to my many museum and conference colleagues for
letting me go on and on and on about change.

SR—
to J, M, and L

to all my co-conspirators in museum work &

to my co-author.

TABLE OF CONTENTS

Exercises to Help Promote Thriving   **57**

Introduction: Why a Guide to Change?

This project grew out of our goal to help others handle change based on lessons we have learned in our respective nonprofit career. We have a combined 40 years of experience in museums. In our time, we have worked alongside scores of colleagues and through numerous changes. We have felt overwhelmed by change but have also found ways to thrive through change. It is from the spirit of sharing that we produced this book.

This book, part theory and part practical manual, is made for anyone dealing with change at work. We wrote this book with our own personal experiences in mind, during what seemed to be an avalanche of change— nationally, institutionally, and in the museum and nonprofit fields. As this personal project grew, a significant amount of research helped us generalize our experiences in ways that we hope will be broadly helpful to all.

The first part of this book defines change and notes its effects on many areas of life, before moving on to the underlying causes of change. The latter half of the book provides exercises and activities you can do to get ahold of change in your life. The experience-based section is split into two sections about change: first, surviving by centering on growing the skills to triage and handle concurrent change, and then, thriving by developing new strategies to move beyond reactionary behaviors.

Throughout, we will highlight recent research into change environments with insight from our own experiences dealing with change. While we both have a background in the museum field, specifically education and publishing in these institutions, we believe our findings are of use for anyone in nonprofits and even the business sector. Working in nonprofits is no longer insulated from the concerns of traditional business practices, and the business press is a wonderful source of research into workplace issues usually derided as "soft skills."

Museums and other nonprofits also are not unique in having a sense of mission that drew people into the field in the first place. Working in a mission-driven institution does have special challenges for the staff of nonprofits like museums, as low salaries and long hours have long been considered the price you paid for working in the humanities. And yet, while museums focus on visitors and communities, sometimes on a shoestring budget, companies like Amazon are famous for their relentless focus on customers while cutting costs as much as possible. Technology and entertainment in tandem are changing not only the idea of museum experiences, but how work gets done inside of them.

We both have written about museums as workplaces in books and blogs and have found plenty special about museums—but many of the changes we're going to describe come from society, focused by the prism of the nonprofit and museum work experiences. We believe that the challenges of working in museums have many parallels which will make this book useful for many readers. The need to take care of yourself at your workplace is universal.

Many workplaces are seeing battles between legacy practices, the sense of "that's the way things have always been done here—and it's the right way," and the appeal of things shiny and new. If you've worked long enough at one place you've probably seen the pendulum swing between change and stability. Indeed, the political upheaval starting in 2016 has been framed as "tradition" vs "change," but strongly tacking back to a so-called traditional past is, in fact, a form of change. Millions of people can feel change from new policies being enacted or the policies of the previous administration being discarded, just as workplaces which may have changed, for example, to be more responsive to digital concerns can feel completely different if those digital programs are cancelled due to budget concerns.

This book takes the position that you are more likely to be in a change environment now than in a stable environment—one way or another, you are feeling change.

So just what do we mean by change? Read on ...

Seema Rao
Robert J. Weisberg

A Note about the Formatting

Sidebars:

Buzzwords:

Like in many fields, new approaches can be full of jargon, buzzwords, and trendy terminology. Words like "design thinking," "mindfulness," and "employee engagement" have been used—and abused—by many individuals and companies trying to solve legitimate problems. As a result, co-workers can become desensitized to new takes on solving old problems, tagging anything which smacks of these approaches as jargon, Emperors with No Clothes, or just plain bullshit which distracts and detracts from the excellence of the company's—or in our case, museum's—mission and the unique work being done in the institution.

While we hate jargon as much as anyone—when used to obfuscate or as double-talk—we disagree that new approaches are antithetical to institutional mission and excellence in scholarship, content, or anything which improves the human condition. So this book uses terminology when appropriate, putting buzzwords *in bold italics*. We ask you to remember the humanistic thinking behind these words and the reason you're reading this book in the first place. Terms will come and go but change is with us now and always.

Defining Change and its Effects

How would you define change? It is the type of term that you innately understand and yet might have a hard time explaining thoroughly. In its simplest terms, change is a move from one state to another. This simple definition, however, glosses over so much of the felt experience of change, like the loss of comfort, the fear of something different, the work required to adapt to a new state, and the actual process of moving from one state to another.

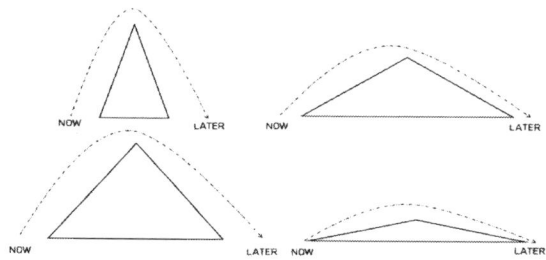

The velocity and scale of change can vary considerably. Time is a particularly important component. As change is as much a perceived experience as a real one, a person might find that a series of small, fast changes can be more unsettling than large, slow ones.

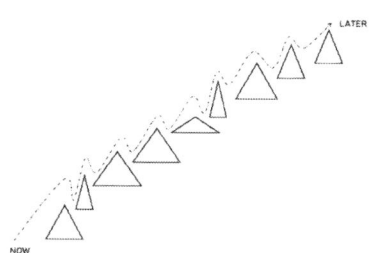

Often, one change will begin a cascade of other changes which cannot be stopped and which can proceed unpredictably. Change, therefore, can be accompanied, with or without warning, by a sense of disorientation as the inputs and outputs we have grown used to no longer apply. This can be exhilarating and yet profoundly unnerving, and you have to expend energy to even to know your place. An unchanging environment where you seem to be standing still is only an illusion, as thinkers as disparate as Gautama Siddharta, the founder of Buddhism, and renowned scientist

Albert Einstein said. Everything is relative, and then we feel caught in the middle, especially when many forces—internal and external—seem to be working against each other. We see this on a personal level in families or groups of friends, colleagues and departments at work, and even political and social forces in our communities and societies. (In the museum field where Seema and Rob work, we've felt this tension all the time between concern for the collection and concern for the visitor, with staff often caught in the middle.)[1]

Over the course of a changing environment, we experience a variety of powerful feelings:

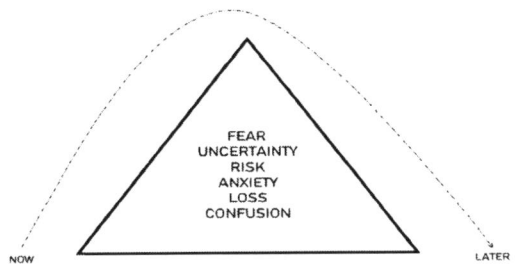

- Risk

- Uncertainty

- Fear

- Anxiety

- Excitement

- Confusion

- Loss

- Anticipation

Books often focus on one of the feelings associated with change. We, however, consider all of these change-precipitated concepts as interrelated. Your experience during change will be your own unique constellation of emotions. Uncertainty about risk itself adds to dislocation and disorientation, increases fear, and manifests as anxiety and assorted other symptoms.

1   Fuentes, Jessica. "The Pushmi-Pullyu of Change in Museums." Art Museum Teaching, 5 Apr. 2017, artmuseumteaching. com/2017/04/06/pushmi-pullyu-of-change/. Accessed 1 Sept. 2017.

These reactions to change have biological roots in our early human minds, which were wired to process change as signals of real and important phenomena both beneficial (seasons, migrations of animals) and harmful (predators). While change might manifest in different ways now than for our ancestors, the results can be just as varied. Changes at work can directly threaten our job status, career, and financial security, and can lead to anxiety, worsen depression, and cause other physical illnesses. In this light, fear of change is a human response to real and perceived stimuli. One should not be embarrassed by fearing change, just as one should not be embarrassed to take care to avoid illness, and once sick, to try to heal. The goal, instead, is to be able to recognize this fear, determine its causes, and move forward in concrete and measurable ways.

The perception of change can be just as debilitating as real change. Even after something positive, we can experience stress over the fear that this thing might be taken away from us or that people might be jealous of our achievement or status. We often become attached to something and anticipate its loss or a struggle to keep it. In this light, a positive change—which itself can be exhilarating, exciting, and stimulating—begins the roller-coaster of emotions that inevitably leads to negative ones like anxiety, fear, and exhaustion. Long periods without change can cause anxiety from fear of looming change, a buildup of tension not unlike the stresses which lead to an earthquake. What these reactions have in common is the eventual feeling of uncertainty and lack of control.

Whether positive or negative, there are long-term psychological effects of change on an individual's well-being. Internal stress is common; unchecked, stress will lead to an external condition like burnout, which can occur for many reasons—when you are facing constant change, doing the same thing day after day, facing career roles that do not meet your expectations, working on too many projects at once, or feeling disengaged in your workplace.[2,3] Burnout—defined here as a psychological inability (which may manifest in physical ways) to continue performing one's current job responsibilities—is an individual reaction to the external stimuli of a dysfunctional workplace and an unhealthy company. You can define health by the level of authentic civility in the workplace,[4] or by how the company recognizes its employees' relationship to others, to their environment, and

2   Garton, Eric. "Employee Burnout Is a Problem with the Company, Not the Person." Harvard Business Review, 20 July 2017, hbr.org/2017/04/employee-burnout-is-a-problem-with-the-company-not-the-person. Accessed 12 Oct. 2017.

3   Seppala, Emma and Marissa King. "Burnout at Work Isn't Just About Exhaustion. It's Also About Loneliness." Harvard Business Review, 11 July 2017, hbr.org/2017/06/burnout-at-work-isnt-just-about-exhaustion-its-also-about-loneliness. Accessed 12 Oct. 2017.

4   Delizonna, Laura, et al. "High-Performing Teams Need Psychological Safety. Here's How to Create It." Harvard Business Review, 24 Aug. 2017, hbr.org/2017/08/high-performing-teams-need-psychological-safety-heres-how-to-create-it. Accessed 1 Oct. 2017.

to society.) While employees should, in theory, communicate how they are feeling to their colleagues, bosses, and even Human Resources, many workplaces do not have enough inherent trust for employees to feel safe communicating in this way. Even though we expect nonprofits like cultural organizations to be healthy places to work—after all, the idea of working in a mission-driven institution and field and avoiding more cutthroat sectors like business or law is what attracts many to the field—an employee may be under such stress that they may not feel strong or secure enough to trust their managers.[5] All sorts of employees can be taken advantage of in nonprofits, but it's often middle- and lower-level staff members who do the hardest tasks, work the longest hours, and lack the power to demand better conditions.[6] Thus, burnout is both cause and effect, the canary in the coalmine and the mine itself. Burnout has to be treated as a company problem—and perhaps an industry problem as well. We'll discuss burnout more later.

Beyond the company level, burnout has many personal ramifications, such as loneliness, a sense that you are the only person doing a given task or the only person doing it well, or that no one understands your work situation. Loneliness becomes both a product of and a driver of burnout. You might become isolated by the forces that cause burnout; similarly, your negative reactions might push people away from you. If you've experienced anything other than a picture-perfect childhood or if you've lived through major, isolating life-upheavals, you know that loneliness can lead to physical reactions.[7]

As we investigate dealing with situations of change, we will return to the concept of *psychological safety*.[8,9] First, we will help you stake out a healthy area of safety in your workplace and life. Then we will provide steps for you to reach and to broaden that place of safety, where the disorientation and discomfort which accompany change can be turned into something that can benefit not only you but your colleagues, community, and the world. We like this definition of psychological safety, from organizational design firm NOBL: "a state in which individuals feel safe sharing their

5   "Five Myths that Perpetuate Burnout Across Nonprofits (SSIR)." Stanford Social Innovation Review, ssir.org/articles/entry/five_myths_that_perpetuate_burnout_across_nonprofits. Accessed 2 Oct. 2017.

6   Timm, Jonathan. "The Plight of the Overworked Nonprofit Employee." The Atlantic, Atlantic Media Company, 24 Aug. 2016, www.theatlantic.com/business/archive/2016/08/the-plight-of-the-overworked-nonprofit-employee/497081/. Accessed 2 Oct. 2017.

7   Eisenberger, N I, et al. "Does rejection hurt? An FMRI study of social exclusion." Science (New York, N.Y.)., U.S. National Library of Medicine, 10 Oct. 2003, www.ncbi.nlm.nih.gov/pubmed/14551436. Accessed 15 Oct. 2017.

8   "Why psychological safety matters and what to do about it." Re:Work, rework.withgoogle.com/blog/how-to-foster-psychological-safety/. Accessed 1 Oct. 2017.

9   Hirsch, Wendy. "Five questions about psychological safety, answered. • ScienceForWork." ScienceForWork, 9 Oct. 2017, scienceforwork.com/blog/psychological-safety/. Accessed 15 Oct. 2017.

ideas with the rest of the team."[10] Since this is a book about the inevitability of change, psychological safety is what allows people the ability to be in uncomfortable situations.

Psychological safety may sound overly corporate, but just think of times when you didn't feel you could speak your mind at the office (the same holds true for families, out in the community, etc.). Here are five questions from a helpful article by John Looney of the enterprise messaging company Intercom.[11] Do you think these thoughts about your workplace?

- If I take a chance and screw up, it will be held against me

- Our team has a strong sense of culture that can be hard for new people to join.

- My team is slow to offer help to people who are struggling.

- Using my unique skills and talents come second to the objectives of the team.

- It's uncomfortable to have open honest conversations about our team's sensitive issues.

Still, be careful that the term psychological safety isn't being used to create a false sense of workplace happiness; instead, interrogate its use until you feel that there is a place where you can authentically be yourself at work.

---

10 Nobl. "How to foster psychological safety on your team, according to this month's Team Ups." NOBL, 7 Mar. 2017, medium.nobl.io/how-to-foster-psychological-safety-on-your-team-according-to-this-months-team-ups-9791836bafc4. Accessed 25 Sept. 2017. This article has a further link to a useful article about Google, which is known for its progressive, if relentlessly-data-driven, goal of constantly improving workplace dynamics: http://futureofwork.nobl.io/future-of-work/why-google-values-this-attribute-the-most-in-teams

11 Looney, John. "Engineering a culture of psychological safety." Inside Intercom, 20 June 2017, blog.intercom.com/psychological-safety/. Accessed 20 Sept. 2017.

Causes, Types, and Effects of Change

Why Categorize ?

Forces of change can feel explosive and ever-present. They are not isolated; instead of a single cause resulting in a single effect, we experience complicated and interacting avenues of change, which can make thinking about change exhausting. Therefore, categorizing the forces of change is helpful to handle uncertainty, to take in a broad and nuanced view of your situation, and to understand how it aligns with the experiences of others. Articulating complex processes are an essential means of investigating and interrogating these elemental ideas and helping you find *authenticity*, defined in a workplace context as more than just "speaking your mind all the time," but as feeling you be your real self at work without fear of reprisal.[12]

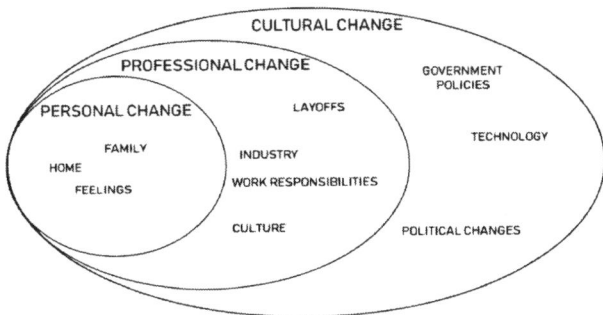

Categorizing change offers you a chance to understand which elements of change are within the sphere of your personal control. Societal or cultural changes involve many complex forces, few of which are in your control—though you can feel more *involved* in the face of what might seem overwhelming. Other forces of change, such as your diet, are much more within your sphere of influence. "Lifehacking" articles on the internet may claim that things such as mindset are easy to fix, but it is also easy to get frustrated.

We are hoping this guide can help you deal with and own such frustration and see it as part of the practice of dealing with change—not something to be fought with, or to beat yourself up with, but to be embraced. How you react to change may not feel in your control, but you can learn to exercise some degree of command. Practice is a constant, just like change.

---

12 Lande, Brad. "Authenticity at Work is More than a Buzzword – Grey Matters – Medium." Medium, Grey Matters, 16 Nov. 2016, medium.com/grey-matters/authenticity-at-work-is-more-than-a-buzzword-6fca2721426f. Accessed 24 Nov. 2017.

A Word about Privilege

From Rob: As an upper-middle-class white cis (as per Merriam-Webster, "a person whose gender identity corresponds with the sex the person had or was identified as having at birth") heterosexual able-bodied male who went to an elite school and landed ("lucked into," itself a problematic self-definition) a job at a prestigious art museum, it took me many years to even understand what *privilege* meant. My secular, suburban Jewish upbringing allowed me a little distance from the dominant American Christian culture—and the stories of distant family who perished in the European Holocaust during World War II allowed me to believe that we could be outsiders in the U.S.—but so many of my friends were Jewish that I grew up with little exposure to anyone different, poorer, or unprivileged. (If someone "only" went to a non-elite public university, it was somewhat of an embarrassment.)

I have been fortunate in the breaks—or lack of bad breaks—that life has had for me, and even more fortunate that a few experiences led me to friends, loved ones, and colleagues with different backgrounds and perspectives from my own. They helped me look at my privilege—and to question how far I was willing to go to interrogate my background and the ease which male whiteness made for my life journey, and how even the hard work of my family and ancestors—done in the face of more difficult circumstances, to be sure—translated into a life made easier by the benefits of whiteness.

From Seema: Privilege, therefore, might be considered a graded scale. As a brown-skinned Asian woman, I certainly can't claim the privilege of whiteness. However, Asians often benefit from their race, associated with positive prejudices of being the model minority. I have certainly been noted for my mathematical prowess and my hardworking ethos. Were these accolades earned or a byproduct of deeply ingrained cultural prejudices? I can't know. However, I can control how I behave. The best I can do is to be honest about my privilege and try not to benefit from it.

Race is but one facet of privilege. Power is born of gender, race, religion, sex, etc. In many ways, being born into the privilege of class precipitated my ability to have the privilege of working in nonprofit. Being a nonprofit employee might not seem to be a privilege; however, I was able to make the choice to work in a low-paying profession for the mission. If food was scarce, or if I had to care for a large family, I could not choose to work in this profession. I never forget that my career itself is a result of the accidental fortuity of birth. I also remember that not everyone in this field has the same privilege. It is important to offer that while many of us in this field come from privilege, some do not. They need all the support we can offer without any of the pity.

This is all to say that we have made an effort—we won't say everyone, because we won't assume my job at this is ever done—to consider the levels of privilege that many readers may not have when developing the texts in part one and creating the exercises in part two of this book. Lack of privilege can make all of the stresses during change more difficult, even life-threatening, and readers may have greater safety concerns than just psychological in the society we live in today. Any lack of speaking to your personal sense of crisis is unintentional and we hope you can build upon this guide, add to it the lessons of your personal journey, and help us build a more change-survivable world.

The following three areas of change are rough divisions, but they do overlap and affect each other.

Personal Change

These are the thoughts and feelings we carry inside—our internal world, our home life, and the interactions with friends and family—and which we feel deeply inside as part of us.

Action, or Choice-Based change can often center around the individual. People might exercise change through choosing educational or career opportunities. Ambition or the need for growth, including financial (necessity or security), can often result in choice-based changes. Even exercising choice can be stressful in response to internal or external situations.

Incremental change operates slowly over time. For example, through childhood, you slowly mature in your emotional reactions. This change might not be apparent from one day to the next. The adult, however, is perceptibly different than the child. Many other personal changes can happen in this incremental manner. You may slowly change into a better communicator or into a stressed parent. Without the long view, you might not notice these changes.

Incidental change is perceived as something that is "out of our hands," where we do not have a choice in the matter. Unlike incremental changes, in retrospect one can point to a moment when this change occurred. However, irrationally, people feel as if the change was outside of their control. (If you've ever done something and then apologized, saying, "That doesn't reflect who I am," you may understand this.) We should examine what these personal reactions reveal about our deeper selves but also realize that one's reactions can have a significant impact on our future.

Life also has a habit of doing its thing. Tragedy and grief are etched on every life in ways universal and unique.[13] Don't apologize for feeling grief, pain, or for having bad days. In part two we'll discuss ways to work through the change which accompanies personal grief, but number one is to permit yourself to feel sadness. One only has to see the difference between Sheryl Sandberg's approach in her book *Lean In*, in which she was criticized for a deaf ear to women who did not have the luxury of wealth to support them as they took charge of their workplaces and careers, and in her follow-up, *Plan B*, where she went to lengths to acknowledge the privilege of her position as she dealt with the aftermath of the sudden death of her husband. Being aware when this happens to others can create atmospheres of compassion which will work in all directions eventually.

---

13 Anderson, Jenny. "Sheryl Sandberg's new book isn't just a memoir on grief, it's a critical guide to reclaiming life." Quartz, 21 Apr. 2017, qz.com/964570/review-sheryl-sandbergs-new-book-option-b-deals-with-her-husbands-death-through-an-intimate-guide-to-grief/. Accessed 1 Oct. 2017.

A Word on Spirituality

Rob, a practicing Buddhist, believes strongly that all things are interconnected and that change is the essence of reality (even if there really is no "I" who is changing!). Seema was raised Hindu, a faith that believes in the universal connectedness of all life. Hinduism is focused on the centrality of the unity amongst all living things, and the ideal of becoming, literally, one with the universe. While this book is not a religious one, We both noted in our preparatory discussions that our faiths underpinned some of our intellectual understandings of change.

In both faiths, we find comfort and validation in all sorts of attachments—physical, mental, digital, seeing a single thing as the answer to all our problems. "The reason desiring causes suffering is because attachments are transient and loss is inevitable."[14] Those in positions of privilege become attached to each thing they can purchase in turn, even if they are ephemeral experiences. People become covetous of the privileges of those above them, of their neighbors who seem to be doing just that much better, or of other socioeconomic groups and races and religions whom they believe get special and easier treatment or handouts. A need to be more spiritual, or to seek out spirituality, can be a profound driver of change—but done authentically it can be a source of strength in dealing with change.

Professional Change

You work hard for the money. But it's hard to stay ahead of change.

Leadership change doesn't just mean a change in leaders, it can mean a change in a leader's vision—sometimes small changes which ripple through the organization. Though societal and technological factors can force change, at your workplace change which most affects you comes from the top. Even a longstanding leader can make changes with profound effects, especially if their vision undergoes a transition into something that many staff members do not agree with.[15] This causes massive uncertainty

---

14 Holiday, Ryan. "The Biggest Threat to Your Success Is the Story You Tell Yourself About Success." Observer, Observer, 20 July 2016, observer.com/2http://hackspirit.com/zen-philosophy-reveals-attachments-lead-suffering-can/016/07/the-biggest-threat-to-your-success-is-the-story-you-tell-yourself-about-success/. Accessed 1 Sept. 2017.

15 Herz, Rebecca. "What does it mean for a museum director to have a vision?" Museum Questions, 19 June 2017, museumquestions.com/2017/06/19/what-does-it-mean-for-a-museum-director-to-have-a-vision/. Accessed 15 Sept. 2017.

and can open chasms in the workplace, even if the changes in vision are for the right reasons, and it's easy to fall in.

A leader can initiate a restructuring, which can cause chaos professionally and personally. New job relationships need to be built, especially if this takes place over a long period of time. Many colleagues may leave, new ones may come in and, in turn, leave in an even shorter time. Everything you'd come to expect from your day, week, month, year, and even career at your workplace can change. And because most reorganizations (or reboots, reorganiztions, rethinks, reconceptions, and so on) are not done well, they require ensuing restructurings to fix or reverse what has already caused so much change.[16] While most reorgs are done in the name of "change," the results often cause more stress than they relieve.

When a team, department, or company gets smaller—or larger, as experienced by many startups—stress can occur around the organization. One of the most common things we've heard after reorganizations or changes in size (from layoffs or hiring binges) from our colleagues is, "I don't know who does anything anymore."

Changes from the top can also be caused by poor quality of leadership. Remember that leaders are workers, too, and may not have been properly trained for the high-level skills they need to practice. (There's no online course for being a visionary!) The changes that occur in a leader's experience— being elevated above colleagues, coming from outside and not knowing the organization, having been hired by executives or a board who themselves may be out of touch with staff members' concerns—may not be easy to handle, and while it easy to say, "they're being paid to be in charge!", training, communication, and trust have to exist and be earned at every level.

Also, just because someone has reached the apex of the organization doesn't mean they are free from insecurities.[17] Leaders set the tone in many ways, and uncertainty from the top can make staff uncertain; employees share their feelings with each other, creating whispers, factions, and back-biting. Strong, confident leaders provide vision, communication,[18] and trust from the top, with the well-being of the entire staff in mind. If change is a constant, a strong leader makes it a positive force to motivate action, not a negative to be resisted. (And yet, even positive change can still require survival skills!) Strong leaders encourage agency and accountability by

16 Heywood, Stephen Heidari and Suzanne Robinson. "Getting Reorgs Right." Harvard Business Review, 10 Oct. 2016, hbr.org/2016/11/getting-reorgs-right. Accessed 5 Sept. 2017.

17 Anhalt, Emily. "The Importance of the Emotionally Fit Founder." Medium, The Mission, 26 Apr. 2017, medium.com/the-mission/the-importance-of-the-emotionally-fit-founder-51558eaf6491. Accessed 15 Oct. 2017.

18 Johnson, Elsbeth. "How to Communicate Clearly During Organizational Change." Harvard Business Review, 5 July 2017, hbr.org/2017/06/how-to-communicate-clearly-during-organizational-change. Accessed 15 Oct. 2017.

demonstrating it themselves. Lack of direction leads to "learned helpless-ness," so expect and demand more consistent signals and behaviors from your leaders, especially when they are leading change! The exercises in part two will help you from a variety of vantage points on the organiza-tional chart.

Digital disruption contributes a great deal to professional change. Our workplaces have been transformed, but not always in a good way. Technology has made many jobs possible but has eliminated many others, some in white-collar fields which required long and expensive periods of education, training, networking, and skills acquisition. We can hire—and become, often unwillingly—freelancers far more easily. Our skills sets at work also become obsolete quickly, except for tasks which seem the most rote and labor-intensive. This is a prescription for becoming bored.

New communication technologies have led to changes in how we interact, and there is rarely a coordinated effort to respect everyone's communica-tion preferences—whether email, phone, IRL, or chat. These misalignments can cause friction and conflict, compounding the lack of communication and trust between colleagues. One article suggests conducting "a network audit to determine how employees across role boundaries connect to each other in person, via email, etc., and what implications this network structure has for feelings of power."[19] Technology can lead to imbalances in collab-oration, where having too much can be as stressful as having too little.[20] Read the exercises in part two about reaching across teams and silos.

Beware the term *disruption* (or even *innovation*), which can be an excuse for pushing people to work harder under more difficult conditions.

Pressures particular to our chosen field can exacerbate feelings of stress during times of change. Seema and Rob come from nonprofit back-grounds, and these institutions can be guilty of crying poverty when sources of funding dry up, or when changes in content consumption lead more peo-ple to stay at home than go to museums. Sometimes these changes are discussed at very high levels and the resulting decisions are not always explained to staff; on the other hand, the staff may notice changes in vis-itorship or user relationships which institutional leaders weren't aware of. (This is why it's a good idea to seek out a variety of viewpoints from your field and to gain perspectives of people in other departments, institutions, and fields—and your customers!)

19 Anicich, Eric M. and Jacob B Hirsh. "Why Being a Middle Manager Is So Exhausting." Harvard Business Review, 22 Mar. 2017, hbr.org/2017/03/why-being-a-middle-manager-is-so-exhausting. Accessed 15 Oct. 2017.

20 Mankins, Michael. "Collaboration Overload Is a Symptom of a Deeper Organizational Problem." Harvard Business Review, 24 July 2017, hbr.org/2017/03/collaboration-overload-is-a-symptom-of-a-deeper-organizational-problem. Accessed 20 Sept. 2017.

Workplaces have also changed in past few decades. The "Mad Men" era is past (or is it?). Progressive workplace practices can be a source of change, or, just as easily, a source of tension when they collide with legacy mindsets—not just from sexism and other forms of discrimination, but the idea of "knowing one's place" or "paying your dues." Sometimes even questioning engagement strategies with the public can cause some professionals in an organization to fear that their place of authority is being usurped. If you like new features being offered, like yoga classes, the eye-rolling of colleagues, especially those in authority, can cause stress.

Superstar coder, technology leader, and US Navy admiral Grace Murray Hopper once said, "On the future of data processing, the most dangerous phrase a [data processing] manager can use is 'We've always done it that way.'"[21] We've heard this many times in museums, but it's true of any legacy, authority-based structure, including families. In museums, it gets said at levels just below the most senior, as fears of scholarly excellence slipping or academic training being rendered valueless push people towards fighting for the old way of doing things. Also, the speed of, and unfamiliarity with, digital- and public-focused rather than lecture-focused educational practices can make specialized scholars fear being left out of the increasingly fast and public conversation over art. Finally, in museums and in academia, lengthy tenure and low turnover can decrease movement within ranks, especially compared to fast-paced departments like digital, design, and education, who are sometimes designated as "support." Workers who are aware of the larger changing nature of work but who experience old-fashioned workplaces can feel especially squeezed between two worlds.

Unfortunately, dysfunctional workplaces can be held hostage by the personalities of the people there, especially managers. And since people's emotional states change, you can experience turmoil merely from the interrelationships between top leadership, managers, and you or your colleagues. Personal politics can be a protean force, as bonds form and reform constantly and become subtle forces of change. Even worse, personality-based change can make us feel especially hopeless because it makes us doubt ourselves and leads to lack of communication and trust, especially towards our senior managers. Many of us want to believe that we are morally above playing office politics (think of the computer in WarGames: the only way to win the game is not to play).[22] But even the best workplaces develop hidden rules and norms at the organizational level;

21 Baldwin, Joan. "Museum Leaders and We've Always Done It That Way." Leadership Matters, 17 Apr. 2017, leadershipmatters1213.wordpress.com/2017/04/17/museum-leaders-and-weve-always-done-it-that-way/. Accessed 31 July 2017.

22 Jarrett, Michael. "The 4 Types of Organizational Politics." Harvard Business Review, 20 Sept. 2017, hbr.org/2017/04/the-4-types-of-organizational-politics. Accessed 15 Oct. 2017.

these unspoken rules can sabotage our attempts to work through changing environments and are also a strong obstacle to thriving in change.

This can be especially hard on middle managers, who have to switch constantly between communicating with the people who report to them and the more senior managers to whom they report. Switching between being a boss and being a follower of senior staff and department leadership creates the same kinds of distractions and mental work of "multi-tasking" which makes the digital workplace so difficult. This article is worth quoting at length:

> "Middle managers … are expected to play very different roles when moving from one interaction to the next, alternating between relatively high and relatively low power interaction styles. By virtue of their structural positions, they are simultaneously the 'victims and the carriers of change' within an organization, receiving strategy prescriptions from their bosses above and having to implement those strategies with the people who work beneath them. As a result, middle managers often find themselves stuck in between various stakeholder groups, which can produce 'relentless and conflicting demands.'"[23]

In this position, middle managers become carriers of change, expected to convey it throughout the organization even if they don't believe in it. And they are often ignored, as modern organizations focus on top leadership or its lowest (and cheapest) levels of labor.[24]

The psychological safety dance is something that all staff members find themselves doing in change situations. It's no surprise that workplaces can have a huge impact on the psychological health of their staff. Though it may seem like a lack of psychological safety is a result of change, we see it as a strong *cause* of change. The decay of safety—and with it, trust[25]—forces us into situations where we feel our ability to work has been compromised. These communication-caused problems with safety and trust take a particular toll on the women, minorities, and other non-cis-het-elite-males. And the effect is cumulative, as lack of safety leads to further communication issues in a negative spiral that requires just as much survival as more obvious change like restructuring or new leadership.

---

23 Anicich and Hirsh. See note 19.

24 "Companies are cutting their lifespans in half by ignoring one type of employee." Quartz, 28 Mar. 2017, qz.com/942824/companies-are-cutting-their-lifespan-in-half-by-ignoring-one-type-of-employee/. Accessed 1 Sept. 2017. (Originally published by Alison Randel on the website The Ready.)

25 Apples, Crisp. "Why is genuine teamwork elusive?." Medium, The Mission, 8 Apr. 2017, medium.com/the-mission/why-is-genuine-teamwork-elusive-f800b408926e. Accessed 15 August 2017.

Good organizations treat psychological safety as a metric, while bad organizations treat it as something that just takes care of itself, a classic communication problem in itself. In fact, some organizations regard a lack of psychological safety as part of the creative atmosphere of excellence! In life-and-death positions like air-traffic control, psychological safety is part of the culture, so that workers get training and improvement when lives are on the line.[26] We're not saying that every job has the same stakes as air-traffic control, but being in a learning environment can help deal with the stresses of changing workplaces. The high-profile disasters and near-disasters (such as the near-crash of an Air Canada jet at San Francisco International Airport in 2017, or the Grenfell Tower fire in London of the same year) shouldn't be the only teaching moments we have. Creating psychological safety for yourself, and working with others to scale up cultures of psychological safety, is the best reaction to, and way to stay ahead of and take benefit of, change.

Vicious cycles lead to burnout. When psychological safety is lacking, and leadership can't find an organizational model that works and is competitive, a cycle begins where change causes more stress which in turn causes more change.[27] The result is that staff become overworked, morale dips, and people leave, causing greater overwork. As communication breaks down, workers lose their connections to their colleagues and become lonely and burned out.[28] Lack of inclusion of non-cis-white-elite-male staff makes this worse.

Baby, You're a Star. Just because you might be a "rock star" in your workplace doesn't free you from stress or the process of change.[29] Again, what seems like it might be a result of change—you're given more opportunities to shine because there's more work to be done or fewer people to do it—can cause shifts in your relationship to your office.

What seems like a "great opportunity" becomes too much when you are counted upon to do the work of many people, by bosses who identify you as the person who has to be in on every project—which can present an opportunity for longer hours and more stress. You might be reluctant to discuss unhappiness with your boss or to demand help, or even to see yourself as someone with any control over the situation. If you're in a

26   MacLellan, Lila. "The ultimate case against using shame as a management tactic." Quartz, 30 July 2017, qz.com/1039957/the-ultimate-case-against-using-shame-as-a-management-tactic/. Accessed 21 Sept. 2017.

27   McKee, Annie, et al. "A 3-Step Process to Break a Cycle of Frustration, Stress, and Fighting at Work." Harvard Business Review, 12 July 2017, hbr.org/2017/07/a-3-step-process-to-break-a-cycle-of-frustration-stress-and-fighting-at-work. Accessed 15 Oct. 2017.

28   Seppala and King. See note 3.

29   Petriglieri, Jennifer, and Gianpiero Petriglieri. "The Curse of Being Labeled a Star." Harvard Business Review, 17 Apr. 2017, hbr.org/2017/05/the-talent-curse. Accessed 1 Sept. 2017.

nonprofit, you may have heard there's no budget for extra pay or for hiring help (though plenty of for-profit businesses use these excuses). You can get identified with the status quo, or you might identify yourself with the status quo and be afraid that change will devalue the talents you believe or have been told are unique to you. On the other hand, if you feel your skills aren't well regarded, you may be afraid that change will expose you as someone who should be fired—this need to constantly prove yourself is sometimes known as "impostor syndrome." You might become attached to a situation at work where you have star status as a defense mechanism against change. Authenticity suffers as we become overly faithful to an identity held by others. Psychologist Carol Dweck, in her book *Mindset*, discusses growth and fixed mindsets—as we become more attached, we become more fixed, and more unwilling to, and afraid of, change.

In the museum field where Seema and Rob have worked, we came up with the term for these stars: "musicorns," a particular kind of museum-field superhero who "does it all for the arts and the visitor."[30] The rock star is especially vulnerable to ending up on too many projects, being asked to give 30 percent of their time on five different projects, or 150 percent total![31] Projects which have nothing to do with each other end up thus connected simply because the (overworked) person gets committed to all of them, and they become the glue holding (or simply sticking) these unrelated parts of the organization together. This is no substitute for a sensibly-organized workplace.[32] In our world, combined with low pay and falling morale, it's driving people out of the field.

Finally, a question you might have asked yourself: what if *you're* the one driving the change? Our answer: just because you started it doesn't mean it's not stressful![33] Whether you created the change situation to begin with in order to get ahead, or you were asked to change something at work, or if you're trying to lead change in your community as a reaction to something else, all of these exercises in part two hold true—and it's even more important to be authentic to yourself, your team, and your organization, no matter the temptations of playing along with power.

---

30 Razzetti, Gustavo. "Why You Need to Stop Being the Superhero and Embrace Vulnerability." Stretch for Change, Stretch for Change, 11 Jan. 2017, blog.liberationist.org/be-vulnerable-to-succeed-in-an-ever-changing-world-6ff4428b64ee. Accessed 15 July 2017.

31 Carmichael, Sarah Green, and Mark Mortensen. "How to Fix 'Team Creep'." Harvard Business Review, 8 Sept. 2017, hbr.org/ideacast/2017/09/stress-is-an-organizational-problem.html. Listened 24 Sept. 2017.

32 Gardner, Mark MortensenHeidi K. "The Overcommitted Organization." Harvard Business Review, 22 Aug. 2017, hbr. org/2017/09/the-overcommitted-organization. Accessed 21 Oct. 2017. This article refers to this workplace practice as "multiteaming."

33 Caddell, Bud. "How to manage yourself when you're managing change – NOBL." NOBL, NOBL, 7 June 2017, medium. nobl.io/how-to-manage-yourself-when-youre-managing-change-e7f2a0522f1. Accessed Oct. 15, 2017.

Change and the Nonprofit World

We have noted many particular change issues at museums and other nonprofits, where the business model can be more difficult to parse than at typical companies and can include:

- Questions about the role of the Board of Trustees

- Disagreements between collection-focused departments like curatorial and public-focused departments like education/interpretation and digital. Curators can feel that the institution doesn't properly give them environments conducive to their research and collection-building, while other departments can feel that curatorial gets too much attention while they are seen as disposable "support" teams. Providing psychological safety to workers who feel that they don't recognize their institution anymore is crucial (especially if both groups feel the other group is favored!); in part two we'll detail some ways that staff can be proactive in taking on this dichotomy.

- The need to improve business practices, as nonprofits can often be run on shoestring budgets and with few real processes in place. This is especially true in environments where funding is threatened or the public attitude toward the work of the institution is contentious. Nonprofits benefit from donations which can stagnate during national and global economic crises. This uncertainty around funding causes more stress during times of growth and retraction in nonprofit organizations.

- Changes in philanthropic behaviors. Younger potential donors, especially if they made their money in technology or other start-ups, are considered more favorably inclined to give to environmental, social-justice, or educational causes than to legacy arts institutions.

Many mission-driven nonprofit organizations are claiming they want to be more transparent, usually meaning with their customers and often in response to public debacles such as airlines have experienced recently. But *transparency* and *openness*, which may become mantras for the customers, don't always translate internally. This gap between what the organization wants for the public and what it does for its staff is another cause of change and a driver of stress.

Societal and Cultural Changes

In 2017 it's impossible to discuss causes of change without mentioning the rapid pace of change in our society at large. While some of these are caused by the march of social technologies and economic shifts, the contested political landscape has pushed change on many people—and had others pushing back, causing change on all sides.

The social impact of technology has upended many people's lives. Social media and smartphones have changed communication, made us always accessible (and always susceptible), distracted us, challenged the underlying nature and security of our jobs, and yet also made great connection and resistance (and many of our jobs) possible. These changes in technology have major ramifications for every field. They can make some processes simpler but can also displace workers. Adopting new technology can be particularly stressful for older workers who are expected to learn, apply, share, and get new technologies funded, without being given extra time at work to do so! The creeping contact commitments of our workplaces—which can border on abusive if we're being reached at all hours, even as we make ourselves more vulnerable to abuse by keeping our phones nearby at all times—can make reacting to change more difficult. In part two, we'll discuss how to use technology in more positive ways.

Changing tastes have affected many companies, including nonprofits. For nonprofits in the cultural sector, competition is coming not so much from other types of culture as much as the desire of audiences to stay home, or only visit museums if they can do so with groups of friends.[34] Traditional media forms have felt the same pressures. These changes can catch entire industries by surprise, and there are not always ways to save these types of professions (ask anyone in print media). Staff can be laid off, and those who remain are often doing the work of several people for the same or less money, causing a further collapse in morale. In addition, as society changes, organizations might be pressured by donors to change. They may be asked to alter hiring processes, for example, or management styles.[35]

---

34 Dilenschneider, Colleen. "Growing Competitor for Visitation to Cultural Organizations: The Couch (DATA)." Know Your Own Bone, 28 June 2017, www.colleendllen.com/2017/01/04/growing-competitor-for-visitation-to-cultural-organizations-the-couch-data/. Accessed 1 Oct. 2017.

35 From the "Managing Organizational Change" conference June 4-5, 2008, http://www.unitar.org/hiroshima/sites/unitar.org.hiroshima/files/5_AF08_WSIII_Managing_Organizational_Change.pdf. Accessed 1 Sept. 2017.

A need to always be positive, even friendly, at work, can be inauthentic[36] and therefore, ironically, a drain on morale.[37] A term for this is "emotional labor"—defined by Olivia Goldhill as "manipulating your own emotions to meet others' expectations"[38]—and it doesn't just exist in customer-facing service industries or visitor-focused fields. This can be emotionally exhausting and reinforces inauthenticity, especially if more senior or protected people seem to get away with being nasty and unprofessional.

We stress for success. There is an attachment to success, especially in the United States, and in the stories we tell ourselves about how successful we are, we become married to these great narratives.[39] In the startup world, rapid change ("disruption") can be a faith all on its own. Real victories start one little step at a time. Don't be forced into changing the world from scratch.

The times are a changin' for cultura l fields. Workers in cultural organizations are well aware of changing demographics: more non-white audiences, millennials, and "attention-compromised" visitors are appearing at our doorsteps, or not, even while governments change their funding priorities and new types of philanthropists have less interest in the arts over more social and environmental causes. These are all causes of stress in nonprofit institutions, which can be seen as ironic since cultural institutions always claim they are seeking new audiences. Speaking to new groups can be stressful for those not trained in unpacking their own privilege (and the privileges inherent in the history of their companies or institutions), and addressing these can lead to the cause …

The elephant in the room is an election where a shocking outcome (though many non-whites have said that they were not surprised) was cast as a fight *against* change, but at the same time represented an enormous change. Because political results are in theory democratic and represent the will of our fellow countrypeople, they have the potential to confound and confuse us, to leave us despairing and defeated, to hurt us profoundly,

36 Lam, Bourree. "The Fear of Feelings at Work." The Atlantic, Atlantic Media Company, 1 May 2017, www.theatlantic.com/business/archive/2017/05/feelings-at-work/524970/. Accessed 1 Sept. 2017.

37 Bennett-Smith, Meredith. "The case for being grumpy at work." Quartz, Quartz, 18 Apr. 2017, qz.com/929348/why-being-grumpy-at-work-is-good-for-you/. Accessed 15 June 2017.

38 Goldhill, Olivia. "Politeness isn't enough; we now demand friendliness. And it's destroying authenticity." Quartz, 1 Apr. 2017, qz.com/947514/politeness-isnt-enough-we-now-demand-friendliness-and-its-destroying-authenticity/. Accessed 20 June 2017.

39 Holiday, Ryan. "The Biggest Threat to Your Success Is the Story You Tell Yourself About Success." Observer, 20 July 2016, observer.com/2016/07/the-biggest-threat-to-your-success-is-the-story-you-tell-yourself-about-success/. Accessed 15 Oct. 2017.

and even to make us consider leaving our homes to preserve our sanity.[40] (Readers only have to look at comments in media from "the other side" after a previous election to confirm that many people can feel this way.) Do you respond with optimism that a democratically-elected figure can and should be resisted? With depression that some of the worst elements of ourselves have been unleashed? Or further optimism that this openness has exposed deep ills in society so that they can be dealt with in the open? (Is optimism a luxury only the privileged can afford?) What about problems which seem to go beyond politics, like global warming? These are truly the change environments which exhaust us, doubly so for people who have experienced oppression in their workplaces and communities (and museums are part of that). It seems that every victory over oppressive histories only causes a firmer reaction. In part two we'll discuss self-care as a radical answer to the reaction to the resistance to oppression, even if you've been part of that history of oppression.

And finally, *change* itself has been a buzzword over the past few years. Terms like "change management," "improved processes," "agile transformation," and "emergent cultures" are heard in every workplace and seen in every workplace-centered blog (Rob knows it is in his blog!). These are often described in strategic plans—but what do they mean for you?[41] If you feel that change is being pushed on you for arbitrary reasons, we want you to know that you can survive that, too; moreover, you can understand why there has been a push for change in your organization.[42] Maybe you're even the person pushing very the change which is stressing you out! In which case, many of techniques for overcoming resistance to change which you might have read about can still be applied to you—perhaps with the help of a friend to ask the questions. Perhaps this guide can be that friend!

---

40 Chancer, Robin. "How To Stay Sane If Trump Is Driving You Insane: Advice From A Therapist." PoliticsMeansPolitics. com, 26 Apr. 2017, politicsmeanspolitics.com/how-to-stay-sane-if-trump-is-driving-you-insane-advice-from-a-therapist-42e982195e22. Accessed 15 June 2017.

41 Little, Jason. "Change Management is Dead." Happy Molly, 9 Mar. 2016, www.happymelly.com/change-management-is-dead/. Accessed 15 Oct. 2017.

42 August Public workshop document, "Inside Out: Tackling Individual Barriers to Organizational Change", workshop attended by Robert J. Weisberg, 26 April 2017.

Why "Surviving" and "Thriving"?

Both of us have investigated and practiced many strategies and techniques for surviving change environments in our work and personal lives. But what we really wanted to do with this book was to move beyond just making it through the low, stressful points—we wanted to pass along ways to make the inevitable changes which you experience work for you, to turn these difficult times into the energy for your own improvement and transformation. The third definition of "thrive" in Merriam-Webster is "to progress toward or realize a goal despite or *because of* circumstances."

We also believe that to truly thrive, you must be able to use your response to change for the benefit of others—indeed, it's hard to think of thriving in a workplace setting if you're not improving the environment around you.

Living through change can feel like you are outside in the midst of a terrible snowstorm. Like living through a wintery blast, you have physiological, physical, and emotional responses to change. To maintain the analogy, for winter, preparations like mittens and boots help you survive the worst of weather. After years of economic difficulties (many people saw little improvement in the "recovery" years after the financial downturn of 2008-9), followed by the 2016 election, reinforced by the constant exposure to news via social media, it seems to many people that all they can do is try to survive a winter that appears neverending.

Yet people do survive winter weather—and learn to make the most of it, to go beyond mere survival, and to actually find ways to enjoy it. Skiing is a useful metaphor for thriving; standing on two implausibly thin sticks, whizzing down slippery slopes and enjoying it. Not a skier? Think about any time when you were able to balance despite the conditions, like bicycling in the rain or wearing dress shoes on a slippery floor. Just as you need to learn the skills to balance for sport or fashion, you can learn the skills to find balance in your life. This book will help you be prepared not only to survive winds (or snowstorms) of change but to be able to grow during periods of change.

The activities in this part of the book are split into the two broad categories of surviving and thriving, patterned after the ideal process for becoming better at dealing with change and transitions. The section on surviving has activities that will help you with the most pressing stresses that occur in the midst of change. With that foundation in place, the section on thriving focuses on new skills that will make you able to take advantage of change, to impart the skills you've learned to others, and to be more prepared for the inevitable changes which the future will bring.

As you go through these activities, be secure in the knowledge that you can do all of these, no matter who you are or what your situation is. If at any time you feel overwhelmed, take a break. At any time during your process, feel free to return to early exercises. For example, during times of stress, you might go back to some of the activities in the surviving section.

Exercises to Help Promote Surviving

The section on surviving focuses on being able to feel strong in yourself during times of change. Surviving can be seen as an internally-focused process. These exercises, therefore, are individually targeted so that you can better handle change at work. Just as you must learn balance before skiing (or biking) in inclement weather, you must learn to balance yourself. You might think of it as being centered even in the midst of the vast storms of change around you.

We cannot emphasize enough that these exercises—and their results—cannot happen all at once. Since survival mode is about dealing with the flight-or-fight emotions of change in the here and now,[43] confronting this can expend a huge amount of mental and emotional energy. More importantly, don't expect instant, breathtaking changes, and don't give yourself a fast deadline for revolutionizing or completely transforming your life.

You can consider the survival section like a form of resistance training, in which you slowly increase the level of difficulty of your work. The Japanese concept of *kaizen* can be useful in framing this small-step process. *Kaizen* can be loosely defined as improving incrementally and continually, like ramping up your ability rather than leaping to a greater state of ability. Small steps allow you to work slowly and methodically.[44]

This approach has an important benefit; it allows you to have numerous small victories, which are proven to boost morale and mood, mitigate the negative effects of change, and let you adjust to growth.[45] As you change your perception of success to focus on the many smaller wins, your motivations will change. You will yearn small wins.

Throughout your work on these exercises, look for and practice small wins, where you've gained clarity for a few minutes, accomplished one calming action during your day, or didn't respond to every attention-destroying email for an hour. Like with any practice, small wins build big, positive habits and become a positive feedback loop to spur your continued success.

We have further broken these surviving exercises into three categories: self-care, time management, and analytical thought. Self-care provides a

43 Kotter, John P., et al. "Survive Thrive." Kotter International, 2017, www.kotterinternational.com/research-and-perspectives/survive-thrive/. Accessed on 15 Oct. 2017.

44 Costa, Rebecca D. "This is the end of risk as we know it." MarketWatch, 12 Sept. 2017, www.marketwatch.com/story/heres-how-risk-as-we-know-it-will-end-2017-09-12. Accessed 29 Sept. 2017.

45 Kramer, Steven J. and Teresa Amabile. "The Power of Small Wins." Harvard Business Review, 8 June 2016, hbr.org/2011/05/the-power-of-small-wins. Accessed 29 Sept. 2017.

sort of "break glass in case of emergency" set of skills for managing your feelings during immediate and difficult change periods. Time management emphasizes useful, but no less urgent, ways of improving your focus and ability to breathe in between challenges in the midst of change. Analytical thought gives you methods for getting ahead of the emotional turmoil of change and lets your brain's higher reasoning take over.

Self-Care

When everything in your workspace is changing, you can feel totally out of control. These feelings have been proven to manifest both physically and emotionally—and your brain often can't tell the difference! Stress can cause headaches, tension, loss of appetite, weight gain, weight loss, exhaustion, blood pressure problems, jaw pain, and digestive issues—in other words, stress can make many parts of your body sick. These symptoms are often coupled with feelings of irritability, anxiety, depression, and hopelessness. This physical and mental combination feeds on itself, creating a vicious downward circle. In the midst of change, you can find yourself too physically and mentally impaired to allow you to react.

This is why the first step in surviving change is to focus on yourself. In times of change that may be the only thing you can control! One important caveat here is to differentiate between *control* and *controlling*. Someone who is controlling takes whatever little power they have, often using this against others. Control is different. Here is where you make clear choices about how you want to act and relate to situations.

In American society, caregiving is most often positioned as caring for others. There are also gender and class ramifications to those acting as a caregiver. As such, self-care can feel unfamiliar for many. Like most people, you were probably not explicitly taught to understand when and how to take care of yourself and your needs. These skills are often not natural and take some practice, especially in workplace settings.[46] Self-management is a set of learned skills where you learn to control how change affects your body and mind. Practicing self-care helps you feel centered and in control. The exercises in the self-care section start with the physical and then move towards the emotional. In practice, you will likely want to attempt activities that deal with the body and mind in tandem.

Another element of self-care is building resilience, the ability to bounce back from the many reversals you will experience in your life— nowadays,

---

46 Su, Amy Jen. "6 Ways to Weave Self-Care into Your Workday." Harvard Business Review, 27 June 2017, hbr.org/2017/06/6-ways-to-weave-self-care-into-your-workday. Accessed 21 Oct. 2017.

you may feel these coming from every quarter, whether directly in your work or family life or more indirectly from the news. Fortunately, studies have shown that resilience can be built up just like a muscle through intentional use (see Exercise 16). And, just like a muscle, resilience needs time to recover after exercise (and merely stopping is not the same as recovering!).[47]

Exercise 1: Decide!

It's very common to put off personal issues during times of change. Avoiding or ignoring self-care can be a form of self-sabotage, especially when you feel you have to prioritize work assigned to you by others. Stress-induced avoidance can manifest itself in many ways, from slowing your progress on tasks to full-on procrastination.

First, it is worth noting that not all avoidance is the same. There are times when you might need to slow down your work. This might appear as procrastination. But, in fact, your instincts are inviting you to take time before setting to a task. This type of apparent behavior often manifests itself when engaging in knowledge-work where you might be synthesizing or creating new ideas. In these instances, your avoidance can actually be productive.

How can you tell when this is a problem? If you find yourself missing deadlines or experiencing other negative ramifications, then you need to modify your process. If you are putting off making decisions, you should spend time building healthier processes.

In order to break this self-defeating cycle, you have to prioritize yourself. This is a foundational exercise for everything which comes after: without making a commitment to do something, you will not be able to make any progress on becoming better at handling stress. Your self-care should flow from an intention to stay connected to yourself. Don't think of self-care as selfish. Instead, consider self-care as a tool to help you maintain yourself so that you can do your job, be available for your family or friends, and follow what is happening in the world. Caring for yourself will have a positive and cascading effect on your life and your ability to live through change.

How?

Try these steps to integrate self-care into your life.

---

47 Gielan, Shawn and Michelle Achor. "Resilience Is About How You Recharge, Not How You Endure." Harvard Business Review, 1 Aug. 2017, hbr.org/2016/06/resilience-is-about-how-you-recharge-not-how-you-endure. Accessed 29 Sept. 2017.

1. Make a verbal commitment to do self-care activities. Promise yourself you will not skip those activities. Studies have shown that repeated stating of a commitment out loud has an important effect on the brain.[48]

2. Use your calendar to help you remain accountable as you perform the activities in the book. Set up meetings with yourself as calendar requests. Mark yourself as out/unavailable; leaving them as tentative would give you an out. This is NOT the same as making a to-do list or putting reminders in your calendar: these are actual meetings you block out, attend, and complete—with yourself!

Exercise 1

Exercise 2: Exercise!

Exercise has many benefits when you are living through change. When you perform sustained, regular exercise, your body releases endorphins, hormones that result in positive emotions. In order words, physical exercise helps alleviate some of the negative mental aspects of change. You can also get tired the right way, which will help you sleep—and lack of sleep strongly contributes to stress.

Along with short-term improvements in your mental state, studies indicate that exercise helps your brain better handle stress over the long-term. When exercising, your body is using many of the same nerve connections

48 Weissman, Jerry. "The Benefits of Speaking Aloud." Harvard Business Review, 23 July 2014, hbr.org/2011/10/the-benefits-of-speaking-aloud. Accessed 15 Oct. 2017.

that fire (and misfire) when you are under stress. Over time, controlled and sustained physical activity will help your body build the ability to use those neural mechanisms efficiently. When stressful times come, your body will be able to handle it like a pro.[49]

There are many ways to exercise. You can start simply at the office by taking the stairs instead of the elevator or walking the long way to a meeting. Even just getting up every half hour and walking around the office can have an important benefit. (Studies have shown that just standing for long periods of time—like at a standing desk—is not the same as exercise. You have to move around! And long periods of sitting can also negate the positive effects of exercise.) Use a timer on your computer, phone, or watch to remind you to get up and walk around regularly. Beyond what you can do at the office, you may want to work out at home or at a gym, or you may prefer team sports. The key for stress management is maintaining a regular routine. Don't try to designate the weekend as recovery-time-only. It's not realistic and just puts more performance pressure on yourself. Remember not to throw yourself so excessively into a new exercise that you hurt yourself!

How?

1. Start by thinking about what are some of your favorite kinds of exercise.

2. Spend time considering the barriers to fitting exercise into your life, either real or perceived. Where do you have gaps during your day, even if just five minutes? Is there a time-wasting activity you do which can be done while briskly walking? (Be careful when looking at a screen during active exercise!)

3. Next, make a plan to break down any barriers. In addition to scheduling exercise, you may need to make space in your life by prioritizing exercise over something else. Is there an activity which is increasing your stress level for which you could substitute some exercise?

4. Finally, find an exercise buddy. This person does not have to exercise with you, though that can be helpful. They should also be in the process of including exercise in their life. This person will help you feel motivated and keep you accountable, and vice versa.

---

49 "Exercise fuels the brain's stress buffers." American Psychological Association, American Psychological Association, www.apa.org/helpcenter/exercise-stress.aspx. Accessed 26 Aug. 2017.

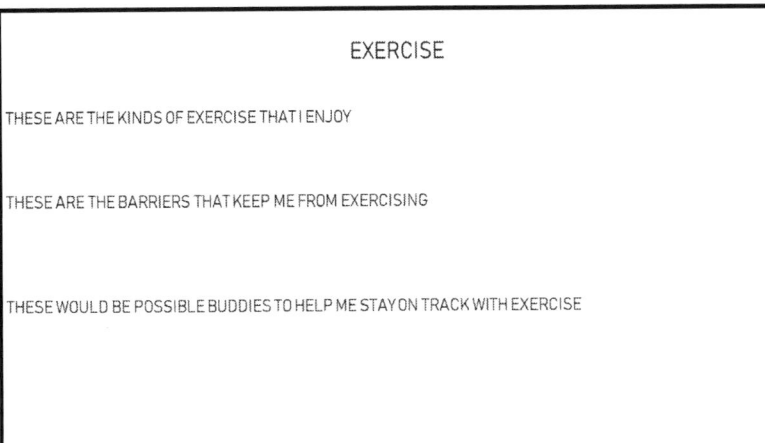

EXERCISE

THESE ARE THE KINDS OF EXERCISE THAT I ENJOY

THESE ARE THE BARRIERS THAT KEEP ME FROM EXERCISING

THESE WOULD BE POSSIBLE BUDDIES TO HELP ME STAY ON TRACK WITH EXERCISE

Exercise 2

Exercise 3: Stress List

Stress is often a concomitant problem to procrastination. As we spend more of our time avoiding the tasks which we must perform, stress can increase. This exercise is designed to help you face stress and break the cycle of avoidance or procrastination. (For a longer discussion of procrastination, see Exercise 1). This exercise is ideal when you find yourself challenged by deadlines or deliverables.

You should do this simple activity regularly, ideally at the same time each day, such as first thing in the morning. This exercise will grow your capacity to avoid procrastination. An important part of this activity is getting stressful thoughts out of your head and onto paper.

How?

1. Start with an empty sheet of paper. (Start with a new sheet each time you do this.)
2. Set a timer for five minutes.
3. Spend 5 minutes writing everything that is stressing you out.
4. Annotate your list as follows:
   a) things that I can do now to cross off

b) things I can change

c) things I can't change

5. Start by doing the things you can cross off.

6. Then, set the timer for 3 minutes. Make a plan for one of the things you can change.

7. What percentage is left on your list? You should find that your long list of stressful items has been culled into a doable set of tasks.

8. Do this each day for a week. Afterwards, try it any time your deadlines or to-dos feel overwhelming.

```
                          STRESS LIST

1. EMAIL............................................DO NOW
2. CHECK VOICEMAIL.................................DO NOW
3. CIRCLE BACK ABOUT BOOK..........................DO NOW
4. WRITE A BLOG POST...........................CANT CHANGE
5. FINISH LITERATURE REVIEW....................CANT CHANGE
6. CHECK IN WITH COLLEAGUES....................CANT CHANGE
7. GO TO STANDING MEETING......................CANT CHANGE
8. WRITE REVIEW OF STAFF.......................CANT CHANGE
```

Exercise 3

Exercise 4: Understand Your Stress

While Exercise 3 helps you triage your short-term stresses, you need to understand the deeper sources of your stress for long-term growth. Once you grow your ability to face stress, you should find concrete and measurable ways to understand its causes. You can handle stress more appropriately once you can make sense of the sources. Through this exercise, you will get a bigger picture of the external forces of stress as well your emotional reactions. Overall, you will be able to see when a stressor is out of your control and when you can make changes to minimize its effects. Ideally, you will also realize that you are not just a "hot mess."

Stress journals can, at first, actually ramp up your level of stress. Do you not take on this activity until you have done the previous three exercsies, in which you examine the most basic effects of stress upon you and signify your commitment to taking care of yourself. Even then, journaling can feel onerous. This activity is set up in a protracted manner so as to maximize insight while minimizing stress.

How?

1. Set aside two days to track your stressors in a notebook. In your notebook, write down everything that feels stressful. For each event, write down:
   a) Your stress level on a scale of 1-10
   b) What happened
   c) Where it happened
   d) Who was involved
2. Give yourself two days before looking at the journal again.
3. After the two-day period, reflect on your entries. Look for patterns. Try to make generalizations; for instance, you might find yourself annoyed when someone suggests that you need to take better care of yourself, especially when it seems they don't understand how much you've already got on your plate.
4. Find ways to break the cycle. For example, put sticky notes in spaces where you experience stress to remind yourself that you are committed to self-care. Send yourself gently-worded emails or set alarms with positive messages—not nags or demands on yourself.
5. Give yourself permission to identify enormous sources of change—societal-level changes, the environment, even long histories in your family or community or nation—and for you not to be able to tackle these large problems yourself. This section is about you.

```
                            STRESS JOURNAL

STRESS LEVEL (1-10)        WHAT?              WHERE?            WHO?

..........................................................................................

..........................................................................................

..........................................................................................

..........................................................................................

..........................................................................................

..........................................................................................

..........................................................................................

..........................................................................................
```

Exercise 4

Exercise 5: Learn the Action of Non-Action

Mindfulness, in its most basic sense, is about noting your thoughts rather than attaching to them. Meditation is one of the most well-known practices associated with mindfulness, which is an expansion of a person's awareness. The key, however, is to make it authentic—just like happiness and positivity, enforced mindfulness for the wrong reasons, and without real meaning, is worse than none at all. You can't be truly mindful if you're just doing it to feel superior to others or to "get ahead" at work.

There is no shortage of books and articles about mindfulness at the office, but organizations with poor communal cultures may see it as a quick fix to make employees happier. However, even if mindfulness is not feasible at the organizational level in your workplace, you can find a supportive community to tap into through research.

Studies show that we are happier at work when our minds haven't gone wandering—one reason probably being that if our work is more satisfying, we are more likely to want to focus on it.[50] Mindfulness is about *being* in the present moment, not recalling, imagining, or examining. It is very, very hard to not let our thinking process run our consciousness, so it takes

---

50 "The Science Behind the Smile." Harvard Business Review, 8 Oct. 2014, hbr.org/2012/01/the-science-behind-the-smile. Accessed 29 Sept. 2017.

work and a lot of self-compassion and forgiveness. A useful definition of self-compassion is provided by psychologist Kristin Neff:

> "the first component of self-compassion is kindness, the ability to shrug off those times when we 'let ourselves down,' when we don't get to check off everything from our to-do lists. The other two components are awareness and, lastly, mindfulness. The goal is not to get more done, but to understand that we are enough and that our worth is not contingent on what we get done."[51]

Forgiveness starts with yourself, and then you can expand to being non-judgmental about others—not because others are incapable of doing bad things, but because judging them in the present moment is attaching you to the bad things they are doing and clouding your ability to be in the present. Again, this is about clarity, not passively accepting wrongs.

With practice, you can learn to choose your actions rather than acting without thought. As Brother Phap Dung, a monk at Plum Village, a French community with a Vietnamese Buddhist center, explains, "Non-action sometimes is very powerful. … Sometimes we underestimate someone sitting very calm, very solid and not reacting and that they can touch a place of peace, a place of love, a place of nondiscrimination. That is not inaction."[52] In other words, there are times where not doing something is more powerful than doing something just for the sake of doing something. Imagine being asked to make an untenable choice. If you refused to make a choice, your inaction would send a message about the overall situation.

In the context of a changing environment, mindfulness helps you focus on the now, not only imagining the future or remembering a nostalgic past.

How?

- Try one mindfulness step every day for a week—note things around you, meditate, or journal. Make sure you note what is happening in the present moment, not what you are remembering from the past or anticipating from an unrealized future. You'll be amazed how much your brain lives in the past and the future!

---

51 Lieberman, Charlotte. "Is Something Lost When We Use Mindfulness as a Productivity Tool?" Harvard Business Review, 25 Aug. 2015, hbr.org/2015/08/is-something-lost-when-we-use-mindfulness-as-a-productivity-tool. Accessed 29 Sept. 2017. Also check out Neff's website: Neff, Kristen. "Self-Compassion." Self-Compassion, self-compassion.org/. Accessed 29 Sept. 2017.

52 Confino, Jo. "A Zen Master's Advice On Coping With Trump." The Huffington Post, TheHuffingtonPost.com, 17 Feb. 2017, www.huffingtonpost.com/entry/zen and-the-art-of-activism_us_58a118b6e4b094a129ec59af. Accessed 30 Sept. 2017.

- See which methods work best for you—maybe you keep the one that's easiest and the one that's hardest. Maybe you'll find that you do better with small bits of meditation during the day than one long sitting session in the morning.[53] The goal is not to add more tasks to your day but to be more present *during* your day.

- Are there patterns you fall into? Can you see when your thinking gets repetitive and plays the same old movie again and again?[54] (This type of self-reflexive exercise requires you to be rational, introspective, and honest. If you feel as if you need help understanding yourself, you can lean on the help of a therapist. However, you can also take up the challenge working incrementally to improve your ability to investigate yourself.)

- What points in your day are you most distracted? Maybe it's when you first wake up, or when you first get to the office and turn on your computer (and check your email). Maybe it's right after lunch or the 30 minutes when you're getting ready to leave (and reading through emails). Make notes for yourself or send reminders to yourself to be more present at those particular times. (And maybe try to get control of checking your email. See a pattern here?)

- After a week, and then a month, see how it's going. Are some reminders driving you crazy? Are you too tired in the morning and just snoozing during your meditation? Is your phone buzzing at you constantly to tell you to calm down? It's okay to look for other methods of mindfulness—this is a very your-mileage-may-vary practice. If trying—and perhaps failing—at mindfulness is making you more stressed, take a step back and look for another way.

- Can you remember a moment in your past when you were particularly present? Maybe it was outside in nature, or looking at a particular piece of art, or experiencing a performance. Maybe you were reading a completely engrossing book. What about that moment put you completely in focus? Write it down and look for similar possibilities in your current situation—or even use that memory to bring you into the present moment.

- If there are times when your work is completely engrossing in a *joyful* way, is there something positive about your work which you can capture and make into a mindfulness exercise?

- Remind yourself *not* to multi-task!

53 Gonzalez, Maria. "Mindfulness for People Who Are Too Busy to Meditate." Harvard Business Review, 1 Nov. 2014, hbr.org/2014/03/mindfulness-for-people-who-are-too-busy-to-meditate. Accessed 29 Sept. 2017.

54 Congleton, Christina and Susan David. "Emotional Agility." Harvard Business Review, 2 Aug. 2016, hbr.org/2013/11/emotional-agility. Accessed 29 Sept. 2017.

- Find a physical location where you can feel quiet and still. It doesn't have to be in complete solitude, but it should be quiet enough for you to be able to loosen the knot of your thoughts. Quiet your phone. Practice being there for one minute, then two, then five, then ten. Remember that this is a place of safety for you in the world.

- Consider an app to help (Rob uses Insight Timer™.) Send yourself random reminders to be in the present moment.

Personal Reflections on Mindfulness

Seema: Mindfulness has been a lifelong challenge of mine. I am an unrepentant multitasker, for example. I am also someone who is prone to need clear, immediate results. My greatest successes with mindfulness came through accepting these parts of myself. You can't change without knowing yourself. So, I started to work on consciously calming myself before starting any mindfulness exercises. I try to sieve off any swirling ideas in my brain by making a Stress List (exercise 2). I might sit and read for 10 minutes. I might step down my level of noise. In other words, I set myself up for success by acclimating myself to a calm state.

Rob: I've been meditating almost every morning now for several years and my mind still wanders! Even though the promises of mindfulness can be oversold,[55] especially when it becomes a corporate mandate, it's been part of my program for being more aware of my surroundings—spending less time in my mind through mindfulness. At work I often use the "Pomodoro" method, which is a 25-minute focused work session, followed by a five-minute break; after several of these sequences, you take a longer break. There are many Pomodoro timers online, and I set up a recurring pair of 25/5-minute countdowns on my phone. But the hardest part is teaching yourself to really work *on one thing* during those 25 minutes! It's a practice, so you need to keep doing it. You should see mindfulness as a path to increasing your emotional skills, not as a solution in and of itself.[56]

55 Goleman, Daniel, et al. "Mindfulness Isn't the Answer to Everything. Here's When It Helps." Harvard Business Review, 28 Sept. 2017, hbr.org/2017/09/heres what-mindfulness-is-and-isnt-good-for. Accessed 1 Oct. 2017.

56 Goleman, Daniel and Matthew Lippincott. "Without Emotional Intelligence, Mindfulness Doesn't Work." Harvard Business Review, 18 Sept. 2017, hbr.org/2017/09/sgc-what-really-makes-mindfulness-work. Accessed 21 Oct. 2017.

Time Management

Once you gain an understanding of your mind and body, you are ready to look at the way that you are using resources. Time is likely your most commonly wasted resource. Think of the number of times when you believed you could accomplish something "quickly" only to realize you had sunk two hours into the task. This occurs because there is a common disjunction between people's perception of and the actual movement of time.

Time management is not solely about being more realistic in estimating how long something takes; time management is also about being in the state where you use your time wisely. For example, when you end up using your time poorly, diluting your attention by switching between many different tasks, you are probably not doing any of them well. In other words, time management also requires improving your concentration, understanding your priorities, and developing good work habits.

The exercises in this section will help you handle these multiple aspects of time management. You can tackle these activities in any order. Many of your negative behaviors are highly ingrained, so plan to come back to some of these activities whenever you need a refresher. They might not seem to work the first time around. But, if you have spent a lifetime dealing with time in a certain way, you cannot retrain yourself overnight.

Exercise 6: Reclaim Your Time

Time is ephemeral. Many of us consistently find ourselves late for one meeting after another. You might feel as if you cannot understand where all your time is "going." In the work environment, often your time is allocated by managers or colleagues, and you never feel that your time is your own. This sense of having something taken from you can cause added stress. Even the shortest breaks, taken for yourself, can create positive and self-affirming energy. This exercise helps you claim respect for your own time by reclaiming moments you might otherwise have "lost."

One of the hardest parts of reclaiming your time is dealing with the distractions of modern life, which are so at odds with concentration. We are constantly finding our focus being eroded by pop-ups, notifications, and alerts. These small breaks in concentration add up, eventually robbing you of considerable time. Studies have shown that even the smallest interruption can require an exponentially greater amount of time to get back to your previous level of focus.[57] This is especially true when you work on multiple

---

[57] Wong, Kristin. "How Long It Takes to Get Back on Track After a Distraction." Lifehacker.com, 29 July 2015, lifehacker.com/how-long-it-takes-to-get-back-on-track-after-a-distract-1720708353. Accessed 30 Sept. 2017.

projects—a single worker can easily spend more than 100 percent of their time added up across all their work commitments!

Think of spending an hour on a task. How much of that time are you actually working? What else might you do? Do not feel discouraged—all you're doing at this point is collecting information about your work habits and styles and how often you are interrupted by your environment. Sometimes, one unstructured hour might be too challenging to maintain on a single task. Structure is an important way to help you increase your aptitude at concentrating on work.

The Pomodoro method mentioned above is one way of teaching yourself to work in a concentrated manner through a structured process. There are many apps and websites that have Pomodoro timers, and there are many variations on this. You'll be shocked how quickly the day can go—and you'll be shocked that meetings need to take longer than 25 minutes!

How?

This is a modification of the Pomodoro method.

1. Chose a multi-faceted project that you need to accomplish.
2. Choose an aspect of that project to work on that requires one set of skills (i.e. research, writing, filing, etc.) Write an intention statement with what you imagine you will get out of this practice.
3. Set aside 30 minutes. Set a timer for 25 minutes.
4. During those 25 minutes, perform only that one type of work. For example, say to yourself, "For these 25 minutes I will only be answering emails." Do what you can to avoid distractions—close your door, move to a different workspace, turn off notifications, put your phone into airplane or do-not-disturb mode, etc. (See the next exercise for more about "digital distractions.")
5. After the timer goes off, take a five-minute break. Try to change your surroundings, like by getting away from the computer. Consider walking around, adjusting your eyes to something different, or chatting with a co-worker or family member (but only for less than five minutes!).
6. Repeat this process again but with a different style of work. At first, you might feel like you can do a few of these "work sprints."
7. Eventually, you will be able to do several of these 25/5 pairs. After two or three "work sprints" make sure to take a longer break of 10-30 minutes.

8. Be realistic! If there is a time or situation where you can't turn off emails, that's okay. The point is to be intentional and proactive in valuing your time and to understand that you work best on a single thing at once.

9. Check your original intention statement and review your time grid. Does your experience match your intentions? Did you find that reallocation of time useful? Would you like to retry this, picking a different time to reclaim?

Exercise 7: Use Digital the "Right" Way

While structure is one way to improve concentration, you will also need to learn new habits. The importance of one's environment is crucial to forming new habits or discarding harmful ones. Technology, from smartphones to computers, can be a constant temptation and can feel incredibly addictive, so complete avoidance can feel overwhelming for some people. In addition, if you work with technology, complete abstinence is not feasible. Instead, try to teach yourself to use technology in a more mindful manner.

How?

1. Spend a week improving your use of technology. Begin by thinking about how you use technology and how it makes you feel. Try to estimate the amount of time that you used it. (Use clues like browser history or social media post timestamps to improve the fidelity of your estimates).

2. Just as you did with your time, journal the use of technology during your day. Note when you feel distracted—do you open a web browser for a quick hit of technology? Do you mindlessly switch to social media? Tally these numbers and create a map of your feelings about using technology.

An example:

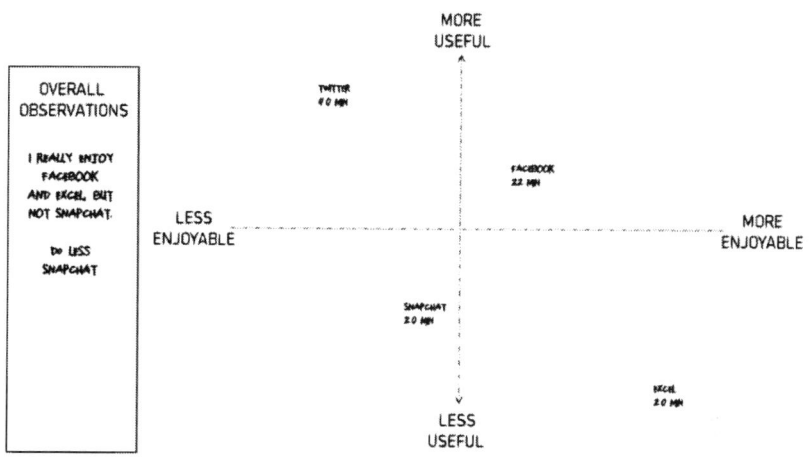

And an empty one for you to fill out:

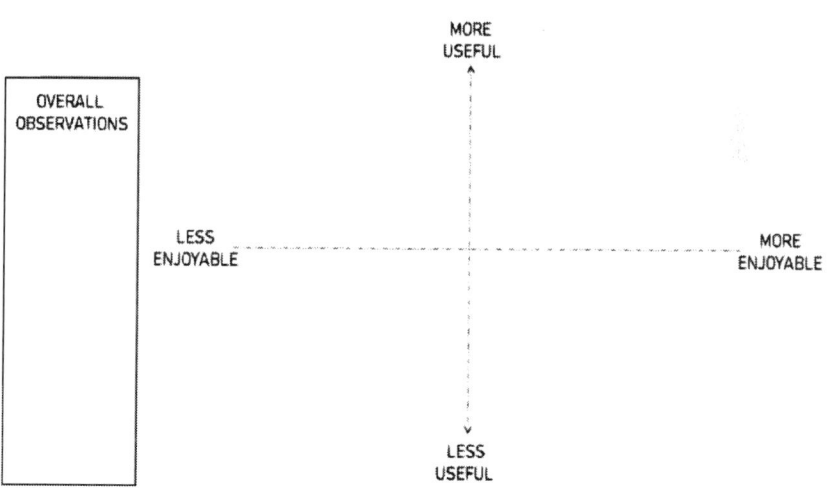

3. Set a smart technology goal that feels attainable. You might set
    a time limit per type of technology. You could also choose to only
    use certain types of technology when at home. You might only use
    social media every other day. You might only cut out answering
    email at night.

4. Spend one week trying to accomplish your goal. You will need to set up ways to support yourself. You can, for example, download apps that lock down social media during a certain period. Or you can turn devices off and stow them away. You can ban smartphones from the dinner table or the bedroom or, if you have the authority, from work meetings! Also, leave notes from yourself to remind yourself of your goals.

5. After the week is over, assess any changes that have occurred. What were your greatest challenges with accomplishing this activity? Don't be hard on yourself. Use this as a tool to help you improve the next time you do this.

6. Repeat this exercise whenever you feel your technology use is adding stress to your life. Leave reminders for yourself to do these tech audits in the future.

Analytical Thought

The previous sections focus on bodily and emotional stability and our relationships to time and respect for our schedules. Once you grow these foundations, you can start improving your ability to consider your options and actions analytically. Just as exercise primes your nervous system to handle the physical effects of stress, practicing analytical thought can help you mitigate cognitive blocks that form during times of change. When paired with mindfulness, the systems in this section help you assess the relative strength of your actions or inactions. Remember that all of these exercises can make you feel worse for a brief moment, perhaps as you realize the depths of your habits to avoid facing reality and being present. This is okay, and part of the healing process.

Exercise 8: Understanding Your Workplace—and Yourself in It

Most workplaces, however small, have an inherent hierarchy. Sometimes, this is codified in organizational charts; other times, hierarchy grows from social capital or informal relationships. These formal and informal channels of power sometimes shift, or the structures of power are more calcified.

Making sense of workplace politics can be helpful both to make you feel more rational in your actions as well as help you find like-minded individuals. Just noting the truths you discover about your organization can help give you a sense of agency. It's important not to let these observations fester into hopelessness but to be a spur to action of some kind—even if just in creating a staff group or sharing with people beyond your immediate circle. It's about not feeling lonely in your knowledge. (We'll get more into working with others in the second group of exercises.) While self-care is individual work, you should remember you are not living in isolation. Talk to your friends and colleagues—you'll be surprised how many of them are facing similar challenges. Finding other people ("finding your tribe") can help you move forward by giving you perspective on larger truths about workplaces. With additional support, you can gain direction on moving towards a more positive place.

How?

1. Start by writing about your workplace. Write as long as you can. Don't limit yourself. Nothing you write is wrong. Don't shy away from judgment. Don't avoid tough subjects.
2. Spend time with your writing. Look for trends in your writing. What are trends that you see? Who are the people you mention? What are the structures that you discuss?
3. Develop a map of the power channels in your organization. How does authority flow around?
4. Now that you have your map, reflect on it. Are there elements of your organization where you might be able to affect change, even on the smallest scales? The largest scales? Where are places where you won't be able to create change? Finally, reflect on ways that you can work with others to make a change. Are there other people you agree with, disagree with?

Exercise 9: Examine Attitudes Towards Change—Yours and Others

Now that you know something about your workplace's structure, it's time to take a look at change in the workplace. There are as many reasons for why people resist change as there are types of change. Knowing the reasons that people resist change can help you understand the feelings in your workplace during times of change—and how these intersect with your own personality.

How?

There are many reasons why people resist change. Look through your previous write-up of your workplace and see which of these apply to situations you've encountered. If there's one particular change you want to focus on, go ahead. Examine this list by Rosabeth Moss Kanter of the reasons people might resist change.[58]

1. Loss of control
2. Excess uncertainty
3. Surprise!
4. Everything seems different
5. Loss of face
6. Concerns about competence
7. More work
8. Ripple effects
9. Past resentments
10. Sometimes the threat [implied by change] is real

Now, do the exercise again, but this time, *apply the reasons to yourself.* Remember, this isn't judging, just noting. The goal here is to find reasons behind people's actions (including yours) and to put them in a larger context of your workplace.

Exercise 10: Drill Down—Communication in Your Workplace

Poor communication is probably one of the most common sources of workplace stress. In times of change, communication breakdowns exacerbate tensions and lead to misinformation, gossip, and backbiting. Communication can be multivalent—across many platforms and by many people. In addition, few people spend time consciously considering their communication weaknesses. Instead, they often focus on the communication challenges of others. This exercise asks you to look at many aspects of communication.

How?

1. Think about workplace communication. Start with yourself. What are your interactions like? Do you prefer phone? Email? A chat app like Slack? One-on-ones? Meetings?
2. Think about the ways that other people interact—which types of communication cause other people stress? What reasons do they give?

58 Kanter, Rosabeth Moss. "Ten Reasons People Resist Change." Harvard Business Review, 7 Aug. 2014, hbr.org/2012/09/ten-reasons-people-resist-chang. Accessed 30 Sept. 2017.

3. Which people whom you deal with make you most stressed? Do you always feel stress with them, or is it most stressful when using a certain form of communication?

4. Identify a less-stressful form of communication with that colleague and circle it. Use that form exclusively (or as much as they allow). For instance, if you find that both of you work better on phone, and they send stressful emails, just respond with a call. (You might still need to send a follow-up email for the paper trail, but note that.)

5. Share your findings with the person in question. Tell them that you have noticed a certain way of communicating is ideal for your work relationship. You may not be able to change the communication styles of others but you can be forewarned and perhaps deflect some difficult interactions into easier styles. People might de-escalate if you just ask them, and they may appreciate the thought you've put into this process.

A Word about Models

There are many models for different styles of workplace communication. One of the most well-known divides people into four quadrants: driver (makes statements, doesn't need small talk), analytical (asks questions), expressive (likes to tell stories), and amiable (likes consensus). These are interesting, and entertaining, and can be enlightening, but as models regularly fall in and out of favor as more evidence is gathered on their usefulness, we're going to avoid such models in favor of exercises. (ENFJ Rob can't get enough of the controversial Myers-Briggs!)

Exercise 11: Dealing with Toxic Individuals and Environments

Workplaces, just like families, are full of all sorts of people, including those who feel toxic. Someone might start out as an office friend but later become someone you can't stand—and even friends might be extremely difficult as co-workers. Others might be universally-perceived as toxic, and yet their behavior has been tolerated or even rewarded, which can have a highly negative impact on workplace culture.[59]

---

59 Sepah, Cameron. "Your Company's Culture is Who You Hire, Fire, & Promote." Medium, Actualize, 3 Mar. 2017, medium.com/goactualize/your-companys-culture-is-who-you-hire-fire-and-promote-c69f84902983. Accessed 21 Oct. 2017.

There is no one way to deal with toxic people and no failsafe formula for saving your sanity. By understanding why some people exude toxicity—they might ask you for more time than you can give them, or they ask for more time than they give you, or maybe they play politics—you can manage your reactions even if you can't avoid these people. For example, you can avoid one-on-one meetings with them.

What's especially problematic is that toxic people can make us more toxic just by being around them.[60] Even the talking-behind-their-back that such people create because of their actions is a drain on time, mood, and morale.

This is not to minimize the impact of people who demonstrate actionable, abusive behavior, especially those in workplace supervisory roles (there's an old adage that people don't quit jobs, they quit bosses, especially as bosses are the people who seem to control future possibilities at the organization). We are not discouraging you from taking action to combat oppression and abuse in your workplace or personal lives; but these steps are designed to help you manage everyday toxicity.

How?

1. Start by making a list of all of the people you see regularly at work.
2. Think about each of those people. What are your emotional first reactions? Does the thought of them make you cringe?
3. Next, consider how much of your time is spent thinking about those people. Do you vent about them to your spouse? Do you have a voodoo doll for that person?
4. Then assess your ability to minimize interactions—especially ones which generally cause confrontation—with that person. Sometimes you can not avoid toxic people, such as bosses, but you structure interactions to be minimal or online. Other times, where you can afford to do so, you can make the choice to cut people loose. In this case, do it whole hog. Remove them from social media, cell phone, etc.

60 Sutton, Robert I. *The no asshole rule: building a civilized workplace and surviving one that isn't.* Piatkus, 2010.

TOXIC COLLEAGUES			
WHO?	MY REACTION TO THEM	TIME SPENT THINKING OF THEM	ACTION NEEDED?

Exercise 11

Exercise 12: Learn Not to Personalize

You rarely have the privilege of completely understanding the people you come into contact with on any given day. You end up constructing a narrative about any interaction based on what you hear, experience, and imagine. Your impression of an interaction is inherently imbued with your own reactions.

People often put a personal spin on interactions with others. Think of a time when you have a bad conversation with someone, and you believed that the other party is mad at you. Then the next day, when checking in with the person, you learn that they were sick or upset about something else. The biggest challenge with personalizing is that it is rarely situated in fact. You can find yourself making situations worse simply by imagining reactions.

Personalizing situations is a natural human reaction and something that you have likely done your whole life. Think of that day in your childhood when you came home feeling like EVERYONE hated you. Undoing these mental habits can be challenging, and you will need to need to be particularly thoughtful to learn new ones.

This is also true with receiving feedback. It can be hard to focus on our actions; instead, we take criticism personally.[61] Hearing about us from

61 Heen, Sheila and Douglas Stone. "Find the Coaching in Criticism." Harvard Business Review, 22 Aug. 2014, hbr.org/2014/01/find-the-coaching-in-criticism. Accessed 29 Sept. 2017.

others is difficult, and always loaded with the other person's biases and judgments. Being able to listen, absorb, and act can build a valuable skill in letting us move on and perhaps even improve from the experience.

How?[62]

1. Start by telling yourself that you will work on not personalizing other people's reactions for two days.

2. After each interaction, let your natural reactions run their course, but then step back and question your feelings.

3. Pick apart the interaction in order to understand what reactions made you feel a certain way. Try to reason out if these feelings come from fears that you might have, such as being unliked, on thin ice at work, etc.

4. Label your emotions (fear, anxiety, etc.). This will help you understand yourself and how much of your negative reactions come from your own feelings.

5. Reassess the situation. There will certainly be times when people are treating you badly. But, when you look at the situation again, without your personal lens, how does it look now?

6. Continue to practice this mental assessment throughout each day. (Warning—this can be tiring!) At the end of this period, assess the difference between your first reaction and your reassessment. This will give you a sense of the scale to which you personalize matters.

7. Periodically go through this exercise until the difference between your reactions and your reassessment is negligible.

62 Boyes, Alice. "50 Common Cognitive Distortions." Psychology Today, Sussex Publishers, 17 Jan. 2013, www.psychologytoday.com/blog/in-practice/201301/50-common-cognitive-distortions?destination=node%2F115855. Accessed 29 Sept. 2017; Boyes, Alice. "7 Tips for Not Personalizing." Dr Alice Boyes - Blog, 22 July 2016, www.aliceboyes. com/7-tips-for-not-personalizing/. Accessed 29 Sept. 2017.

Exercises to Help Promote Thriving

The section on thriving focuses on building upon your area of psychological safety and learning new skills to be flexible and proactive during times of change. Thriving is a word that has growth connotations—in the medical sense, a thriving child is someone who is growing both emotionally and physically. In the workplace, a thriving employee might be seen as someone who is emotionally and physically able to grow to handle challenges without burnout. This is also a person who is equipped to be able to handle current challenges in order to develop a better future.[63] When you're thriving, you're taking the survival lessons and using them on the environment around you, learning and growing; as opposed to surviving, thriving is about making and taking advantage of opportunities.[64]

When you are in thriving mode, you are also able to share the lessons you are learning with others in positive, constructive ways. In fact, as you begin to thrive, you may insist on being in an environment that supports this mindset, and see a workplace which discourages growth as being not worth your while. Having moved past survival, you will have the self-assurance to support others on the path. As you go through these exercises, try to think of ways that you can share your process with others.

Reframe[65]

Frames are constructs by which people make meaning of the world around them. These frames vary from person to person and are heavily influenced by their upbringing, culture, outlook, and personal opinions. The frame is a cognitive tool to create split-second understanding of any situations. Frames are mutable and change as one gains more experiences. If in childhood, you have a negative reaction to a certain situation—say you always get a cold when you camp—your frame of reference for camping will be negative.

Reframing is a useful tool to change your natural reactions to situations. In many ways, reframing is about teaching your brain to see a glass as half full after a lifetime of seeing the glass as half empty. This tool is particularly useful when trying to unlearn knee-jerk negative reactions. Adding

---

63 Porath, Gretchen and Christine Spreitzer. "Creating Sustainable Performance." Harvard Business Review, 8 Oct. 2014, hbr.org/2012/01/creating-sustainable-performance. Accessed 29 Sept. 2017.

64 Kotter International, "Survive and Thrive." See note 43.

65 Breazeale, Ron. ""Positive Reframing" as Optimistic Thinking." Psychology Today, Sussex Publishers, 25 Sept. 2012, www.psychologytoday.com/blog/in-the-face-adversity/201209/positive-reframing-optimistic-thinking. Accessed 29 Sept. 2017.

positivity to your outlook, through acts of kindness and generosity, can give you currency which you can spend later.[66]

These techniques are also often associated with positive-thinking theories. Happiness, for example, can be fostered by focusing on the positive aspects of any situation. In this instance, it is important to see happiness and sadness as not being mutually exclusive. A happy person is someone who can learn to handle sad situations and find happiness where they can. What's important for each individual is to find what provides them with *meaning*, which can endure even in times which cannot be happy, and *purpose*, which brings that sense of meaning into the future.[67]

Happiness itself is a slippery idea. With the premium on happiness in our society, many people find themselves "faking it" or pretending to be happy. The state of happiness is exceedingly individualized and hard to define. Some scholars suggest that you look for the ways that others define happiness to help you make your own definition, but don't let this activity lead to a feeling of inadequacy if you feel that your definition doesn't measure up! In terms of reframing, you might start by moving away from "happy" and think instead about positive feelings—take stock of what simply makes you puts you in a positive frame of mind. Nothing is too small for this list. Think of the moments when you feel good, even if you wouldn't call them "happy moments." This might be the time you spend in the shower, that moment you ate the best french fries ever, or the time you spend with your partner. Taken cumulatively, this can be seen as a benchmark for your sense of happiness.

It is especially important to understand that happiness cannot be forced onto others. While you are going through your reframing exercises, be careful not to inculcate others into your own personal "cult of happiness." People need to take their own path through change, and people can get annoyed if you push emotional reactions onto them.

---

66 Kopans, David. "How to Evaluate, Manage, and Strengthen Your Resilience." Harvard Business Review, 24 Apr. 2017, hbr.org/2016/06/how-to-evaluate-manage-and-strengthen-your-resilience. Accessed 29 Sept. 2017.

67 McKee, Annie. "Being Happy at Work Matters." Harvard Business Review, 26 Oct. 2016, hbr.org/2014/11/being-happy-at-work-matters. Accessed 29 Sept. 2017.

Change-Makers

The type of growth mentality discussed in this book sometimes goes by the term *change-making*. Many of the exercises in the thrive section are in line with the ways that change-makers think. This term has become a buzzword in many fields, similar to disruption; but we see it as how, at the most basic level, someone works to push for new and better processes within their field, their organization, or even just their department. They look for places for improvement and find constructive ways to enact this change. The exercises in the thrive section follow a similar methodology, though focused on your own place within an organization. Performing these exercises will help you strengthen your own ability to not only thrive during change but also grow into a change-maker.

That said, the role of change-maker (also known as the "change agent") is a challenging one, even in the most protean and flexible work environments. The change-maker is a person who serves as catalyst and engine of change; they can gain the rewards of credit but also the blame for challenges. Therefore, this contested role is not one to be engaged in lightly. Ideally, in order to foster change, the individual should have a strong internal scaffolding of self-support. If not, the exercises in the survive section can help them.

Exercise 13: No Superpowers Required!

Nonprofit workers often join the field due to a personal attachment to an organization's mission. The office culture often encourages long hours, with many staff performing multiple roles. Often, the organization might claim that there is no funding for additional help (a.k.a., "more with less"). Eventually, many staff members feel that improving the working conditions at their jobs are not an institutional priority. Either way, with so many people seeking these jobs, staff members often feel unable to argue about workload or salary.

In this type of environment, especially during times of organizational change, you can easily take on too much work. Colleagues might be leaving, jobs might be terminated, or roles re-arranged—but all the work has to keep getting done, and we all know what that means. You might feel compelled or forced to do it all. The steps below will help you to not demand so much from yourself (to know what's possible and reasonable for you to do) and to trust in others (especially if you are a manager).

How?

1. Spend some time writing out the answers to the following questions:
   a) What do you do well?
   b) What parts of work makes you feel positive emotions?
   c) What parts of work make you feel negative emotions?
   d) When are you not kind to yourself, i.e., when do you take on more work than you know you can handle? Why?

2. Assess your answers. Do you see any patterns?

3. Next, reconsider your answers based on these questions:
   a) Are there times when you could assuage unhappiness by reframing the situation? Could you change any statements from "must" to "could"? Or from "should" to "shouldn't"?
   b) Are there times when you should/could say no?

4. Make a plan to put one or two of your reframed statements into action.

5. After a few weeks, go back to your notes. Did your reframing work? Are there a few more reframed ideas that you would like to put into action?

6. Consider making a user's manual—to yourself.[68] It would include information about you like your working style, what you value, what you don't have the patience for, how to best communicate with you, how others can help you, and what people misunderstand about you.

Exercise 14: Make It about the Team

Harnessing networks will make dealing with times of change so much easier—for you and others and your organization. Even if you start with the intent of making this about individuals, the company will benefit. People who are proactively learning how to thrive during change will have a vested interest in sharing their process with others. Their change-adaptability is better supported in a fostering environment, which provides a positive feedback loop. Supporting others, therefore, can be an act of self-care.

---

68 Fessler, Leah. "Completing this 30-Minute exercise makes teams less anxious and more productive." Quartz, 9 Aug. 2017, qz.com/1046131/writing-a-user-manual-at-work-makes-teams-less-anxious-and-more-productive/. Accessed 1 Oct. 2017. The organizational culture company August also had a podcast devoted to making a user manual to yourself: "A Manual for Working With Me." August Public, 8 Oct. 2017, soundcloud.com/emergentagenda. Listened 10 Oct. 2017.

If you remember the earlier exercise about toxic individuals, this is your opportunity to improve the psychological health in your workplace by not tolerating—and especially not rewarding—jerks on the team.[69]

Unlike many other exercises in this book, this one is best done with a group of colleagues—you will really need the perspectives of others to come up with insights about your organization. You risk myopic views of your workplace if you rely only on your own views. This can be a trust-building exercise as well. (Trust us!)

How?

1. Work with your to team, or close colleagues, and begin by considering your organization:
   a) Is the organization putting the efficiency of your group over your humanity?
   b) Are you being listened to?
   c) Are you not being respected?

2. Ask these questions in reverse—are *you* respecting the humanity of those in your team? Are you listening to them?[70] Are you respecting them?

3. Consider how your organization handles change. Is change communicated well? To all staff? Top down? Is it transparent, open? Do some people seem to know what's going on and others left in the dark? Brainstorm all the things that seem to be lacking in how your organization handles change, and note different opinions from members of the group—it might indicate inconsistent communication patterns in your organization.

4. Next, individualize this for your working team. Work in pairs. Explore how the challenges in your organization manifest in your working group and individually with each member of the group. Consider how your own personal change aversion might be causing friction.

5. Now, look at all your findings. As a team, interrogate your assumptions. How many of these can be reframed? What is gained when you reframe these situations? For example, let's imagine that your team has to move offices. You might first find that this change is detrimental due to its distance from public spaces.

69 Sutton, Robert. "Building the civilized workplace." McKinsey & Company, www.mckinsey.com/business-functions/organization/our-insights/building-the-civilized-workplace. Accessed 21 Oct. 2017.

70 Folkman, Jack and Joseph Zenger. "What Great Listeners Actually Do." Harvard Business Review, 1 Oct. 2016, hbr.org/2016/07/what-great-listeners-actually-do. Accessed 29 Sept. 2017.

But, in the practice of reframing, you could also consider that the distance from public spaces allows your team more opportunity to concentrate.

Exercise 15: Work on Your Resilience

Resilience is your ability to take the circumstances that are besetting you and bounce back from these challenges to make them into growth opportunities. The study of resilience has been growing in the business world, expanding on the old-fashioned ideas of "grit" and "toughness," particularly in environments that prize adaptability. Resilience skills are often forged in the fires of change, and while they are useful for surviving change, they are particularly suited to help you grow and thrive. This exercise is the beginning of a long process to grow your resilience. *Harvard Business Review* offers a number of other resources on the subject of resilience.

How?[71]

1. Think of a moment that was very stressful. Spend some time thinking about why it was stressful and how you reacted.

2. Next, think of three concrete ways that this situation could have been worse. Be realistic—not every problem results in World War III. What could have gone more wrong?

3. Reflect on how you would have reacted in each of those worse situations. How much do your imagined reactions differ from your actual reactions? How were they similar?

4. Now, this is important—what could you have done after your *real* stressed reaction to have given yourself time to recover and recharge? Did you go right into another stressful situation? Did you mean to take time off but ended up working through it?

5. Plan on a rest and recovery period from your use of resilience. Write down a time when you will not dwell on a work or personal difficulty—and in keeping with small wins, make it short, even a minute. Then, with the knowledge that most problems could have been worse, plan on longer stretches of recovery in the future.

---

71 "A quick therapeutic exercise that boosts emotional resilience." Mark Tyrrell's Therapy Skills, 21 Mar. 2016, www.unk.com/blog/quick-therapeutic-exercise-that-boosts-emotional-resilience/. Accessed 29 Sept. 2017.

```
┌─────────────────────────────────────────────────────────────────┐
│                          RESILIENCE                             │
│                                                                 │
│  A STRESSFUL MOMENT                                             │
│  · · · · · · · · · · · · · · · · · · · · · · · · · · · · · · · ·│
│                                                                 │
│                                                                 │
│  THREE WAYS IT COULD HAVE BEEN WORSE          REACTIONS        │
│  · · · · · · · · · · · · · · · · · · · · · · · · · · · · · · · ·│
│                                                                 │
│                                                                 │
│                                                                 │
│  POSSIBLE REST AND RESILIENCE STEPS · · · · · · · · · · · · · · │
│                                                                 │
│                                                                 │
└─────────────────────────────────────────────────────────────────┘
```

Exercise 15

Exercise 16: Radical Acceptance

Building upon the mindfulness practice of the previous section, you can extend your observation of your internal state to situations around you. Again, this doesn't mean you approve of what you encounter, or that it's right—but that you accept its reality. Accepting the death of a loved one is a particularly significant example; accepting layoffs in your workplace is a more measured version.[72]

This doesn't mean denying your disappointments, fears, anxieties, and pain, but it means not focusing on those reactions, and not building upon them. You are accepting reality and building on that reality—perhaps creating a response in which can confront that reality and take action to change it in the future. You aren't saying "okay" to something bad—you are saying "okay" to yourself so you can respond and move on.

How?

The practice of radical acceptance is a lifelong one. This activity is meant to start you on your path.

---

72 Hall, Karyn. "Radical Acceptance." Psychology Today, Sussex Publishers, 8 July 2012, www.psychologytoday.com/blog/pleces-mind/201207/radical-acceptance. Accessed 29 Sept. 2017.

1. Think of a situation when you felt totally out of control. Describe that situation.

2. Now think about how that situation came to pass. What was your role in making this event occur, or in not preventing this outcome? What about the role that others played?

3. Were there parts of this situation where you were in control during the lead-up to the outcome? What about after the situation? You are looking for times where you could have exercised some agency.

4. What was your response? How did you feel?

5. How did your response color your feelings about the people and places involved in the situation? Think about friends, family, strangers.

6. Now, imagine going back in time—but now, focus on accepting the way things are. Could you have moved on earlier? Saved yourself excess stress and dwelling on the outcome?

7. Do you feel that this acceptance is something you can practice in the future? If not, why not? Again, using the idea of small wins, is there a small situation you can practice on?

RADICAL ACCEPTANCE

DESCRIBE AN OUT OF CONTROL MOMENT

MY ROLE IN THIS

WHEN WERE YOU IN CONTROL   HOW DID YOU FEEL?

BEFORE

DURING

AFTER

REIMAGINE THIS MOMENT FOCUSING ON RADICAL ACCEPTANCE

Exercise 16

Envision

Envisioning is similar to reframing in that you attempt to change the way that you see something. However, envisioning is about using imagination and play to develop new outlooks. While many of the reframing exercises involve emotional introspection and can even be tinged with challenging insights, envisioning should feel light and enjoyable.

Exercise 17: Develop a Personal Vision and Mission

Most nonprofits have a mission and a vision statement. The mission is, in essence, what they do. The vision statement encompasses their greatest aspirations. Developing your own guiding principles can similarly help you through change. A personal vision and mission serve as a compass to help you know where you own true north is.

How?

1. Begin by making a list of your achievements. Why do you value these? What were your motivations for doing those things? Were they internal or external?
2. Next, write down a list of adjectives that describe who you *really* are.
3. Finally, finish the following:
   a) I stand for....
   b) I am best at....
   c) I hope to....
4. Set aside your notes. After a break, revisit your notes. Now try to fashion your notes into a statement:
   a) What is your foundation? (mission)
   b) How will you rise to your best self? (vision)
5. Once you have created two succinct statements, take some time to render them in an attractive way. You can do this digitally or by hand. Just create something that appeals to and contains meaning for you.
6. Place these signs in places that you will see them every day. Maybe carry a small version with you so you'll see it often and know it'll be close by.
7. Finally, how can your sense of mission and vision impact other people? Without proselytizing, think about ways in which you can impart your clarity to your workers, customers/users/visitors, etc.

Exercise 18: Map Your Own Journey

Change can be hard in part because a path you might have originally planned on taking no longer exists. This exercise is meant to help you focus on being able to forge your own path, independent of the changes of your organization.

How?

1. Start with the notes and journaling exercises that you have done in other exercises. Look at the ways your reactions have changed through this process.

2. Borrow a page from colleagues in the user experience (UX) or other user-facing research groups in your organization. (If your institution doesn't have one, reach out to friends—chances are you know someone in this field. You can also look online for customer/user journey maps.) Create a journey or "heat map" (a table which uses intensity of shading or color to indicate greater frequency) of your stressful interactions in the office and in your community. What are the pain points, the spots you dread in the process? Can any of these pain points be removed? Can your organization, colleagues assist?

3. Spend time reflecting on your change journey. What are some places where you need to continue to grow? Where have you been particularly successful in dealing with change? What tools and mindsets were most useful to you?

4. Consider the people on your journey. Who gives you positive energy? Who sucks it away like a vampire? You might not be able to avoid every negative person, especially if they're a supervisor, and you don't want to be inauthentic, but you can make accommodations to yourself to avoid situations which bring out the worst in you.

5. Taking your journey map as your starting point, make a plan for your future growth during change by using some of the exercises in this book or by researching new ones.

Here is an example of a journey map already filled out:

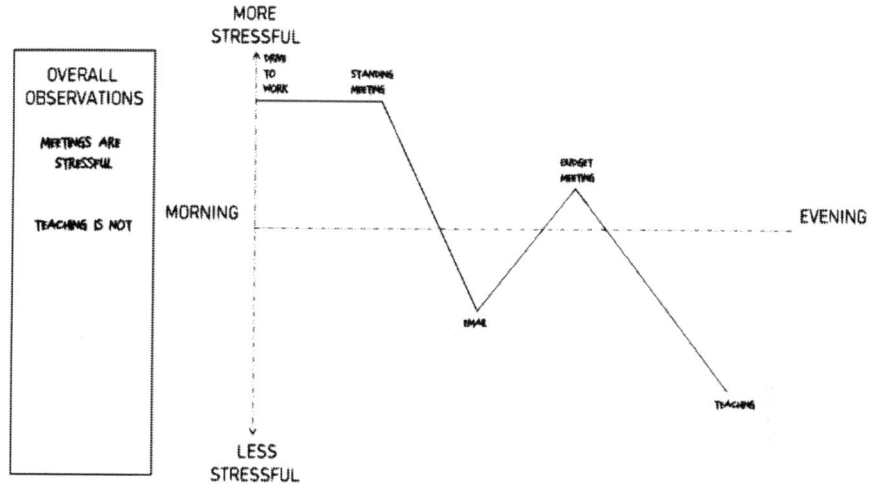

Here is a blank example for you to fill out:

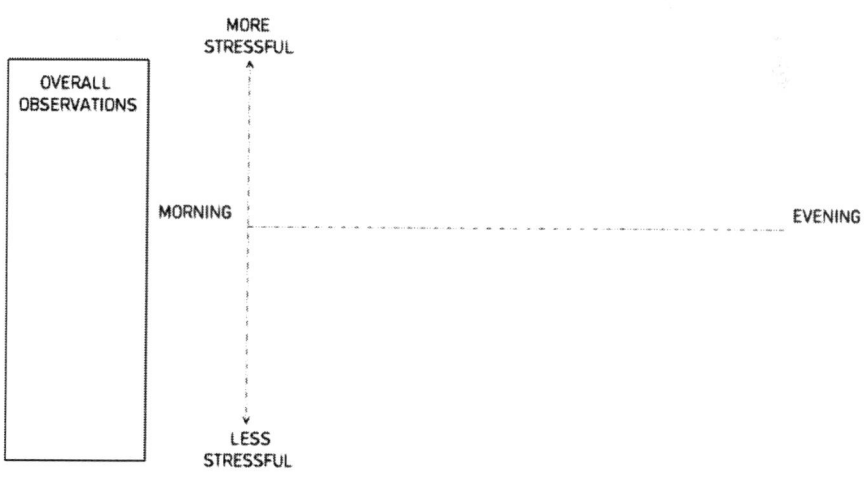

Exercise 19: Deconstruct Your Surroundings

Just as you can try to use visual models to understand yourself, you can use these tools to investigate your organization. Trying different cognitive tools—in this case, using visual meaning-making rather than textual—can help you uncover different insights.

How?

1. Map your organization on a large piece of paper. Make sure to highlight the relationship of individuals and the hierarchy. Don't be afraid if the drawing is messy—it's more likely that this reflects your organization than it does your drawing ability!

2. Try to develop a sentence that describes your organization as a complete system. (If you want to read more about systems thinking, you can start here.[73])

3. With that in mind, draw the large factors which impact the organization (funding, visitor trends, etc.). What forces cause change? Try to define the flow of each of those changes as a series of if-then statements. For example, "If we don't make our fundraising goals, then less money is available for staffing. If less money is available for staffing, then staff is laid off. If staff members are laid off, then there is more work for the people who remain. …"

4. Now go back to these processes and try to reconstruct your statements. Your answers have been based on previous views and experience. Try to reframe your answers by breaking assumptions with an open mind. This is a good place to see the interconnectedness of many different processes. (If you're looking at the surroundings of a situation outside of work, this can be even truer.)

5. With all your new findings in front of you, attempt to reconfigure your organization in ways that feel like a better system. (Start by defining what "better" means to you.) Then consider how each change will make your organization better. Finally, what can you do to bring these changes about? Again, start with small wins!

6. And now, thinking back to psychological safety, is there a place of trust and safety in this organizational map you've drawn? If so, can you become more of a part of it? If not, can you help create one?

---

73 Acaroglu, Leyla. "Tools for Systems Thinkers: The 6 Fundamental Concepts of Systems Thinking." Medium, Disruptive Design, 7 Sept. 2017, medium.com/disruptive-design/tools-for-systems-thinkers-the-6-fundamental-concepts-of-systems-thinking-379cdac3dc6a. Accessed 1 Oct. 2017.

Example of a possible organization map:

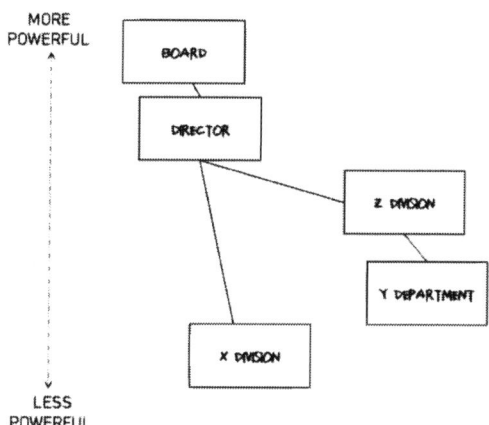

Exercise 20: Change as a Game

If change is considered a movement from one state to another, you can almost imagine your life-like game board—some actions will result in your moving forward, others back. One of the greatest challenges in dealing with change is uncertainty, since so many changes seem to come at you out of nowhere (though on a deeper analysis you can see how they might have been predicted or at least prepared for). Board games, with their finite beginning and ending, manage uncertainty.

How?

1. Choose a project or experience for which you have a certain beginning and ending, such as pursuing and completing a graduate degree

2. Draw out a game board, in the vein of games such as Chutes and Ladders, Candy Land, or Life, with all your hopes and fears included. The act of drawing this out in and of itself helps you create some order out of your fears.

3. Take out dice and play your game. Do it a few times. Each time you will hit different spots on the board. Think through each of those paths. How do they feel? What would do if your path turns out to be that way?

4. Life will likely be different than any toss of the dice, so don't take the game too literally. This activity, however, offers a structured way to consider the paths you might eventually take—and the many ways in which change can come at you. Such activities allow you to grow self-empathy (see Exercise 22) and focus on positive action during change.

GAME BOARD

GAME NAME

GAME PLAN

Exercise 20

Act

While change can be stressful, inertia can be equally challenging. Many of the exercises in this book focus on interior thought and planning. However, at some point, if you do not act, you can become frustrated. This section offers some activities that will help you thrive during change by taking action.

Exercise 21: Acting for Growth

Actions can be large or small. Either way, action-based change benefits from a feedback loop. As you gain positive feeling and success with changing your behavior, you will want to try other changes; but, if you have setbacks, practice self-compassion and be kind to yourself. Try again. Start small! Don't try to change the world all at once.

How?

1. Go back to the very beginning of the book. Look at some of the issues that stressed you out. Brainstorm some lifestyle changes that you could enact to break through the stress. For example, if you are stressed about having an administrative job, how can you add creativity in your life?

2. Set a 30-day goal to try that activity. Make a reasonable goal. Take this seriously. Don't miss the appointments you have made with yourself. For example, draw for five minutes a day, or do some other practice that is tangential to your work, in small-enough increments that you can it do it even during busy periods or times of stress. Make daily appointments on your calendar to get this done.

3. At the end of 30 days, assess what you have learned, especially about yourself, during this process.

4. Think about the next action you can take. Can it be a little bit larger than what you just did?

```
┌─────────────────────────────────────────────────────────────┐
│                      GROWTH JOURNAL                         │
│ MY 30 DAY GOAL                                              │
│                                                             │
│ KEY STEPS                                                   │
│                                                             │
│                                                             │
│                                                             │
│                                                             │
│ PROGRESS (CROSS OFF DAYS AS YOU FINISH)                     │
│  1 2 3 4 5 6 7 8 9 10 11 12 13 14 15 16 17 18 19 20 21 22 23 24 25 26 27 28 29 30 │
└─────────────────────────────────────────────────────────────┘
```

Exercise 21

Exercise 22: Radical Empathy[74]

There are as many definitions of *empathy* as there are contexts in which to consider it. Merriam-Webster's is a useful starting point:

> "the action of understanding, being aware of, being sensitive to, and vicariously experiencing the feelings, thoughts, and experience of another of either the past or present without having the feelings, thoughts, and experience fully communicated in an objectively explicit manner; also : the capacity for this"[75]

Psychologist and researcher Daniel Goleman definies three different kinds of empathy: cognitive, emotional, and empathetic concern.[76] Before we disappear too far down this rabbit hole, however, it's probably more useful to think of what what empathy *isn't*. Empathy is not simply attempting to "feel as others feel." You cannot do that authentically. Rather, focus on the mindset that fosters empathy—just asking yourself how you would feel and what you would do *if you were in another person's situation* places you in that mindset. You can accept that you can never completely understand another person's feelings, but the more you understand the history of someone else's situation, the better you can feel and act in an empathetic manner. Remember that you should maintain your practices of self-care. Empathy can be exhausting—but so can loving and caring for others!

There are many articles taking the position that empathy does not scale—you cannot empathize with the entire world at once, or a large group of people cannot empathize at once, or an institution cannot empathize the way an individual person can. There is also a belief that by focusing on others in very different situations than ourselves, we expend too much energy imagining experiences we cannot possibly understand, rather than taking immediate action within our own experiences (and that empathy, like any mental process, is a finite resource).

For the purpose of this guide, we accept that there is an active discussion around the strengths and limits of empathy, but we ask you to consider that an attempt to empathize is the first step towards understanding others with compassion (which can be thought of as a more generalized type of caring

---

74 Segran, Elizabeth. "Try This Exercise In Radical Empathy To Minimize Conflict." Fast Company, Fast Company, 21 Dec. 2016, www.fastcompany.com/3066609/try-this-exercise-in-radical-empathy-to-minimize-conflict. Accessed 29 Sept. 2017.

75 "Empathy." Merriam-Webster, Merriam-Webster, www.merriam-webster.com/dictionary/empathy. Accessed 24 Nov. 2017.

76 "Empathy 101." Daniel Goleman, 13 Oct. 2013, www.danielgoleman.info/empathy-101/. Date Accessed 24 Nov. 2017.

for others without necessarily trying to understand their internal suffering).[77] And we want to emphasize that compassion starts with oneself, and that compassion and mindfulness are not the same things. Practicing empathy can make at least a part of your workplace better![78] Like with mindfulness, don't take for granted that empathy is a magic, instant solution to all workplace problems.

A misunderstanding of empathy is that it's all about inhabiting the minds, feelings, and emotions of other people. In fact, the first task in being more empathetic is to improve *ourselves*—how well we listen, understand, think about other perspectives, and connect what others say they need to what we can provide for them.[79] Empathy, like compassion, when properly practiced, starts in contemplation but leads to action, which is what thriving under change conditions is all about.

How?

1. Remembering back to the play-nature of previous exercises, think of a situation where you can play the role of someone with whom you might have conflict. Write out your assumptions about their motivations and reactions.

2. Explain to this person that you are having a hard time seeing their point of view. Work together to find a place where you can experience something they do. For example, if they have a terrible meeting, ask if you can join them (though don't interrupt or negatively impact them.)

3. After that experience, reflect on your original assumptions. What has changed?

4. Use those thoughts to improve your interactions with that person.

5. If you're a manager, you have a special obligation to be empathetic and compassionate to those who report to you. (Though keep in mind that a desire to not hurt someone's feelings can sometimes lead us to be inauthentic.) This can be difficult if you're a middle manager. Work on listening and not interrupting, and not zooming ahead with your own brilliant response, no matter how

77 Ovans, Andrea. "What the Dalai Lama Taught Daniel Goleman About Emotional Intelligence." Harvard Business Review, 4 May 2015, hbr.org/2015/05/what-the-dalai-lama-taught-daniel-goleman-about-emotional-intelligence. Accessed 29 Sept. 2017.

78 Blumenthal, Dara. "Research Shows 3 Ways to Bring More Humanity to the Workplace." Entrepreneur - Start, run and grow your business., Entrepreneur, 21 July 2017, www.entrepreneur.com/amphtml/297441. Accessed 21 Oct. 2017.

79 Goleman, Daniel, et al. "The Focused Leader." Harvard Business Review, 9 Nov. 2016, hbr.org/2013/12/the-focused-leader. Accessed 29 Sept. 2017.

well-intentioned. This is your opportunity to improve the world just a little bit.[80]

6. Try this exercise again at a later point—has empathy become any easier to practice?

Exercise 23: Becoming a Workplace "Intrapreneur"

This final exercise builds on many parts of the book, particularly the analytical thought and reframing section. In this activity, you try to change your approach from being an employee to being an *internal entrepreneur*. During times of change, sometimes the best response is to consider starting the change yourself.

In the nonprofit world, you can find small elements of your job or organization that you can impact with an entrepreneurial spirit. An entrepreneur is strategic and big-picture oriented, not afraid to make mistakes and learn from them. They are willing to take action and accept risk. In terms of change, basically, they are making change happen rather than letting change happen to them.

How?

1. Start by picking a market opening, place, or practice in your organization where you can make change. Be thoughtful to work within your own sphere of responsibility.

2. What's already there in the organization? What skills do your colleagues already have? What "small wins" have people already made? Check first before re-inventing the wheel—you might find your great idea is already being done, but you can help bring it to people's attention! It's a marker of resilience that people can use their skills they already have to overcome problems in new and original ways.[81]

3. Now, look at the market, or organizational, need from the point of view of an entrepreneur. What are the opportunities? View all of the activities that occur as part of this from this lens. Develop a new vision.

4. Who is your team on this? (You didn't think you'd be doing this all yourself, did you?) They don't all have to be in your division—or

---

80 Keltner, Dacher. "Avoiding the Behaviors That Turn Nice Employees into Mean Bosses." Harvard Business Review, 8 Sept. 2016, hbr.org/2016/10/dont-let-power-corrupt-you. Accessed 29 Sept. 2017.

81 Coutu, Diane. "How Resilience Works." Harvard Business Review, 11 July 2016, hbr.org/2002/05/how-resilience-works. Accessed 29 Sept. 2017.

even in your institution. Sometimes, having helpers or sponsors outside your group can provide an important perspective.

5. Make sure there's psychological safety in this team—don't practice the negative things you've seen from bosses and others just because it seems like these people get ahead. Make the team a place of trust.

6. Now engage the team in your vision. Reaching out to others will actually effect change. *Real and lasting* change starts from below, not from the top! Pay attention to the silent team members, and engage them in a conversation around whether they feel comfortable contributing.

7. Put your plan in action. Be strategic in your roll-out. Innovate as your role out your plan. Assess, learn, and improve.

8. Once you make your plan happen, spend some time reflecting. Compare your reflections with those of your colleagues. Failure can teach as much as success. What would you do next? Entrepreneurs look to grow and then move on to the next thing.

Note that this exercise hasn't mentioned bosses. While we're not pushing you to go rogue (you may have heard "it's easier to apologize than to ask permission"), entrepreneurial undertakings always carry some risk of disapproval from the chain of command—all the more reason to be in a place of psychological safety before moving on to intrapraneurship! Think of your team first; you'll be surprised how an atmosphere of trust can spread outward through an organization.

Conclusion

Rather than a conclusion, think of this a commencement. As you complete these exercises, remember that you are just at the beginning. You have completed something that required energy and time. You might have faced emotions that were challenging. You might have felt uncomfortable. So, what next?

First, be proud of the work you have done. This book was written to foster active engagement and positive transformation in the face of change. Along with these exercises, you should also feel an underlying mindset in the book that encourages reflection, honesty, action, and acceptance. Hopefully, you have found you have more ability to handle change.

You should also be realistic about the future. This book will not inoculate you against the negative effects of change. You will likely find that you will cycle between just trying to survive and flowering under change. These reactions are normal. As noted in the Defining Change and its Effects section, everything is in motion all the time, so you will often find yourself trying to get your bearings. This book can be a helpful tool to revisit as you find yourself stressed.

Now you find that you have moved from stasis or a stress state onto a different, more constructive path. Yet you are just a few steps down the road. It's an opportunity to take stock. We provided a large number of exercises to give you many paths to seeing yourself in different growth situations. What types of exercises most appealed to you? What types of exercises felt the most impactful? You can use these answers to help you find your next methods to explore for handling change. For example, the mindfulness meditation might really appeal to you. This topic was introduced but not explored fully in this text. There is a wealth of literature waiting for you. You might instead find that this book helped you get the point where you feel good, and you do not want to do more. This is also okay. There is no one right way to handle change.

Change is around you constantly. It can be exhausting, draining our emotional energy, taking time away from things which give us joy. In a way, we're asking you to step into the change, to be the car that steers into the skid or the ship that turns into the wave. We hope our discussion of surviving gives you a place to start, and that our description of thriving inspires you to reach out to and find others in the same situation and start building reserves of strength.

You can react mindlessly, or with practice you can find ways to take action in the face of change. In the latter, you are in the position of being able to make the choice of your actions. In the end, we hope that this book helps you get to this point: where you feel like you can be able to survive and thrive no matter what change storms around you.

Most of all, we hope you see that to change is human, and to sense change being thrust upon you is human, too. To react and survive, to grow and thrive, are what we keep us human.

Thank you for reading. We want to keep this discussion going. Please reach out to us on Twitter at #ChangeSurvivingThriving, or individually at @artlust (Seema) or @robertjweisberg (Rob). We'll take it from there.

Use these pages for notes

Printed in Great Britain
by Amazon

87349874R00047